THE SECRET LIFE OF BEES

Sue Monk Kidd

AUTHORED by Adena Raub
UPDATED AND REVISED by Adam Kissel

COVER DESIGN by Table XI Partners LLC
COVER PHOTO by Olivia Verma and © 2005 GradeSaver, LLC

BOOK DESIGN by Table XI Partners LLC

Published by GradeSaver LLC, www.gradesaver.com

First published in the United States of America by GradeSaver LLC. 2008

GRADESAVER, the GradeSaver logo and the phrase "Getting you the grade since 1999" are registered trademarks of GradeSaver, LLC

ISBN 978-1-60259-165-3

Printed in the United States of America

For other products and additional information please visit
http://www.gradesaver.com

Table of Contents

Table of Contents

Biography of Kidd, Sue (1948-)

Sue Monk Kidd was born on August 12, 1948. She grew up in Sylvester, a town in southwest Georgia where her family had lived for two centuries, on the same plot of land where her great-great-grandparents had lived. The stories her father invented for her as a child and the encouragement of her English teachers fueled her desire to become a writer, yet her uncertainty about her future as a writer, combined with the "cultural climate of the South in 1966," prompted her to pursue a nursing career instead. She graduated from Texas Christian University in 1970 and spent the next decade working as a registered nurse and college nursing instructor. Also during that time, she met and married her husband, Sanford "Sandy" Kidd, and together they had two children, Bob and Ann.

Sue Monk Kidd was just shy of her thirtieth birthday when she finally turned again toward a writing career. She wanted to write fiction, and she enrolled in writing classes at a local college. Unexpectedly, her innate gift for writing nonfiction surfaced when a personal essay written for a class appeared in *Guideposts Magazine* and was later featured in *Reader's Digest*. Thus her freelancing career began.

Kidd gained recognition quickly. She became a contributing editor at *Guideposts*, and throughout these formative writing years she published numerous articles in *Guideposts* and in various journals and newspapers. It was also during this time that she discovered the writings of Thomas Merton and C.G. Jung, whose work she cites as having a deep impact upon her spiritual life and writing. Her first two books, *God's Joyful Surprise* (1988) and *When the Heart Waits* (1990), were spiritual memoirs depicting her introduction to contemplative Christian spirituality and her subsequent spiritual transformation.

In her early forties, Kidd's spiritual journey led her in an unanticipated direction: toward the "sacred feminine." *The Dance of the Dissident Daughter* (1996), her third and most evocative spiritual memoir, chronicles her path to "feminist enlightenment."

Despite the success and acclaim she enjoyed writing spiritual nonfiction, Kidd's desire to write fiction begged to be fulfilled. Refusing to give in to her fear of failure, she immersed herself in the process of writing fiction by taking a graduate writing course and attending various writers' conferences. Soon the author accumulated several awards for her short fiction, giving her the confidence she needed to begin writing her first novel, *The Secret Life of Bees*, in 1997. Lily Owens' story has touched and inspired readers since its release in 2002. Kidd tells a compelling tale of Owens' determination to find the mother she never knew and her coming of age, both physically and spiritually, in the house of the beekeeping Boatwright sisters during the height of the Civil Rights movement in South Carolina.

While Kidd has said that *The Secret Life of Bees* is largely a product of her imagination, elements of the author's life are interwoven into the story, such as the bees living in the bedroom walls, the hair rollers fashioned out of grape juice cans, and Kidd's relationship with the sacred feminine. The novel spent over two years on the *New York Times* bestseller list, has been published in over twenty languages, and is being taught in high school and college classrooms across the country.

Kidd's second novel, *The Mermaid's Chair* (2005), won the Quill Award for General Fiction. Also set in South Carolina, it is the story of Jessie Sullivan, a married woman in her early forties who falls in love with a monk and finds herself torn between her husband and her soul mate, unsure if the mythical power of the mermaid chair is the cause.

In 2006, a collection of Kidd's early inspirational writings titled *Firstlights* immediately landed on the *New York Times* extended bestseller list. As of late 2008 there were more than 200,000 copies in print.

Kidd has been awarded numerous distinctions for both her nonfiction and her fiction, including the 2004 BookSense Book of the Year in paperback for *The Secret Life of Bees*. She is on the board of advisors for Poets & Writers, Inc., and she is the Writer in Residence at The Sophia Institute in South Carolina. She currently resides near Charleston, South Carolina, with Sandy Kidd and her black lab, Lily. Sue Monk Kidd is certain that she will someday write another memoir because she "still [has] a need to create a narrative of my life. To keep writing it until I see how it turns out."

About The Secret Life of Bees

The Secret Life of Bees is Sue Monk Kidd's first novel, following several acclaimed works of nonfiction. The novel follows Lily Owens in the summer of 1964 in South Carolina. On a quest to discover her mother's past, Lily travels to a honey farm in Tiburon, South Carolina. There she discovers the Boatwrights in a fabulous world of beekeeping, spirituality, and obsession with honey. Lily discovers more about herself, her mother, and society than she could have imagined before she began her journey. She learns about the power of females not only as individuals but also as they work collectively.

In an interview with *La Vie en Rose*, Kidd confesses that very little of Lily's existence relates to her own childhood. She insists that her father is the exact opposite of T. Ray, and she adds that while Lily merely wanted to go to charm school, Kidd actually did go. Kidd did, however, grow up in the South in the 1960s, giving her a sense of the paradoxes of the region. While Kidd insists that none of the characters in the novel is based on any specific person in her life, she acknowledges that at times people she knew speak through her characters.

The novel began as a short story that Kidd wrote in 1993. Several years later, she began a three-year process of converting the short story into a novel. To inspire her creativity, Kidd put together a collage of photos that she thought would relate to the plot of the novel. Though she was not exactly sure how she would connect all of the photos, she included a pink house, three African American women, and a wailing wall.

In order to write the book, Kidd also spent extensive time in a honey house and observing beekeepers. Kidd told BookPage that these experiences were necessary to create the sensory stimulation in the novel. "I could never have gotten that from a book. The fear and delight of all that and the sounds of it," she says. Kidd developed the figure of Our Lady of Chains from a statue that she discovered on a trip to a South Carolina monastery. She told BookPage that she was captivated by the story of a masthead of a woman that resurfaces from the depths of the sea.

A *New York Times* bestseller, *The Secret Life of Bees* earned tremendous acclaim from a variety of publications and endorsements from numerous novelists. A British publication, *Woman and Home*, discussed the book as a "superb rites of passage novel." Susan Isaacs, author of *Long Time No See*, called *The Secret Life of Bees* "compulsively readable." The book was awarded the Literature to Life Award, and an excerpt from the novel was included in *Best American Short Stories*.

The book also has been developed into a film adaptation released in October 2008. The film stars Dakota Fanning as Lily Owens, Queen Latifah as August Boatwright, and Alicia Keys as June Boatwright.

Character List

T. Ray Owens

T. Ray (Terrence Ray) is Lily's father, though Lily cannot bring herself to call him "daddy." He is a poor excuse for a father, abusive and unloving. He has turned bitter after the death of his wife, Deborah, and he often takes out his anger on Lily. T. Ray's upbringing is a mystery in the novel, but he owns a peach farm. He employs Rosaleen to assist in taking care of the Owens household. Lily's job is to sell peaches for him at a roadside stand, though the customers are few and far between. August tells Lily of a time when Lily's mother gushed about how wonderful T. Ray was. Lily ultimately realizes that T. Ray must have had a great love for her mother, and that when she left, he developed ill will. At the end of the novel, he realizes that keeping Lily in his house would just remind him of Deborah, so he leaves her with the Boatwrights.

Rosaleen Daise

Rosaleen is the Owens' black housekeeper. Her age is unknown, but she is from another city in South Carolina. She is a spunky woman who deeply cares for Lily. She does not take abuse from anyone, and she ends up getting arrested as a result of her rebellious nature. Lily breaks her out of jail, and the two of them travel together to Tiburon, where they meet the Boatwrights. Rosaleen becomes fast friends with May Boatwright, and she easily joins the routine of the household. Yet, she encourages Lily to come clean with August, even if it means they will have to abandon their new life in Tiburon. Throughout the novel, Rosaleen acts as a motherly figure toward Lily. She provides thoughtful advice or a well-timed pat on the knee. Rosaleen promises to stay by Lily's side no matter what she encounters.

Lily Owens

Lily, the novel's narrator, is also the story's protagonist. Lily begins the novel at age fourteen, a sad girl who has experienced far more than most have at her age. She lives in Sylvan, South Carolina, with her father, T. Ray, and her housekeeper, Rosaleen. Lily's mother died when she was just four years old, and Lily has a confusing memory about the day that she died. As far as Lily remembers, she shot her mother by accident, which is never denied throughout the novel. She is ridden by guilt, loss, and confusion about her mother. T. Ray tells Lily that her mother, Deborah, actually left them. Lily disagrees and runs away. She and Rosaleen escape to Tiburon, South Carolina, because Lily found this city scratched into her mother's picture of a black Mary. Using the black Mary picture, Lily and Rosaleen end up at the Boatwrights' house, the owners of the Black Madonna Honey company. Lily lies about her background in order not to alarm the Boatwrights. The Boatwright sisters welcome Lily and Rosaleen to stay with them, provided that Lily helps with the honey processes. Lily loves her life in Tiburon, keeping bees, and keeping her life a secret. While living with the Boatwrights, she meets a black boy named Zach, with whom she falls in love. Zach is the first black boy Lily has been attracted to, and eventually he kisses her. Lily realizes that she must come clean to August Boatwright about her background, so she explains everything about her past. In addition, August explains that Lily's mother had stayed at the Boatwright house long ago as well. Lily learns the whole story of her mother's past, and she is filled with anger, pity, and grief. She eventually comes to terms with her feelings. Finally, T. Ray comes to the Boatwrights' house to take Lily back to Sylvan. Lily persuades him to let her stay with the Boatwrights, with whom she realizes she has many mothers.

Avery Gaston

Avery Gaston is a police officer nicknamed "Shoe." He arrests Rosaleen for pouring snuff spit on three white men's shoes. He allows the white men to beat Rosaleen both outside and inside the jail.

Mrs. Henry

Mrs. Henry, Lily's teacher, helps Lily realize her potential to do more than go to beauty school. She encourages Lily to pursue her interest in writing in order to begin a career in writing or in academia.

Brother Gerald

Brother Gerald is the Owens' family minister. He finds Lily and Rosaleen resting in his church when they are on their way to town. He is clearly uncomfortable by the idea of a black woman accompanying a young white girl.

Snout

Snout is the Owens' family dog.

Deborah Owens

Deborah Owens, formerly Deborah Fontanel, is Lily's mother. She grew up in Richmond, Virginia, where August Boatwright worked as her housekeeper. As an adult, Deborah moved to Sylvan, following a friend from high school. She dated T. Ray and only agreed to marry him after she discovered she was pregnant with Lily. After a brief term of happiness following Lily's birth, Deborah's life turned dark. She left T. Ray and Lily to live with the Boatwrights. After shaking her depression, Deborah went back to Sylvan to take Lily. During this foray, she and T. Ray got into a fight, which resulted in four-year-old Lily picking up a gun and accidentally shooting Deborah, killing her.

August Boatwright

The owner of the Black Madonna Honey company, August is a black woman who grew up in Virginia. She studied at a black college and became the housekeeper for the Fontanel family. She went on to become a teacher, but when her grandmother left her the beekeeping yard, she moved to Tiburon to manage the honey company. August has a true love for bees, for life, and for love. She offers her help and advice whenever she can, and she becomes a stand-in mother for Lily. She is a spiritual woman with some eclectic hobbies and customs.

May Boatwright

May, August's and June's sister, also grew up with a twin sister named April. When the two of them were small, May would duplicate April's symptoms. If April got a fat lip, May's lip would swell as well. April suffered great depression, and when she turned fifteen, she killed herself. As she grew older, May's empathy grew to encompass the struggles and pain of the world at large. May found great sadness in the pain of others. When an unpleasant or sad topic would be brought up in a room, she would hum, "Oh Susannah" and leave. She built a wailing wall as a catharsis for her pain, but she remained unable to bear the weight of the world. She ultimately took her own life as well.

June Boatwright

June is August's and May's sister, the quietest of the three. June worked as a teacher for a while and then worked in a morgue. She then began playing the cello to comfort people as they die. At the beginning of Lily's stay at the Boatwright house, June resented her because she had resented Deborah. June did not like August working in a white household. Yet, June came to love Lily. June also is in love with Neil but refuses to accept his marriage proposal for most of the novel. She was left at the altar by her first fiancee and therefore is nervous about entering into a marriage agreement again. Yet, eventually, after May's death, she is convinced to marry Neil.

April Boatwright

April was May's twin sister. She suffered severe depression and at age fifteen committed suicide, which changed May forever.

Neil

June's boyfriend and eventual husband, Neil attends most of the Boatwright family functions. He is persistent in asking June to marry him, but she continually rejects him. Finally, following May's death, June accepts Neil's proposal and marries him.

Daughters of Mary

Queenie, Violet, Lunelle, Mabelee, Cressie, and the Boatwrights are a group of women who worship Our Lady of Chains (Mary). The women are close friends, and they share in each other's joy and pain. They eventually welcome Lily with open arms and include her as one of them.

Otis Hill

Sugar-Girl's husband, Otis is considered to be the one male "daughter of Mary." He attends all of the Daughters' events.

Zachary Taylor

Zach is a black boy who works on the honey farm assisting August with beekeeping. He is smart and is a talented football player. He has aspirations to become a lawyer. After he meets Lily, the two of them become fast friends and subsequently fall in love. After Zach is jailed for a crime he did not commit, he becomes angry and becomes concerned with civil rights. He devotes his life to changing the world. Among his first steps in that direction is his decision to attend a white high school.

Clayton Forrest

Clayton is a white Tiburon attorney who teaches Zach about law. He works to defend Zach when he is jailed, and he helps Rosaleen and Lily avoid criminal charges in Sylvan. He is the father of a girl named Becca, who is friends with Zach.

Jackson

Jackson is a friend of Zach's. He throws a soda bottle at a white man, landing himself, Zachary Taylor, and two other boys in jail. Jackson refuses to confess in order to free the others.

Eddie Hazelwurst

Edie Hazelwurst is the police officer who questions the Boatwright family and Lily following May's death. He encourages Lily not to lower herself by living with a black family.

Willifred Merchant

Willifred Merchant is a writer from Tiburon who has been recognized with Pulitzer Prizes for her books about the deciduous trees of South Carolina. The city of Tiburon devotes a day to her each year.

Jack Palance

Jack is a celebrity rumored to be visiting Tiburon. He supposedly planned to bring a black woman with him to the movies, causing much uproar and protest in the city.

Miss Lacy

Clayton Forrest's secretary, Miss Lacy gives information to T. Ray about where to find Lily.

Judge Monroe

Judge Monroe is the Tiburon judge. He is out of town when Zach is jailed, which delays Zach's release.

Melvin Edwards

Melvin was June's first fiance. He left her at the altar.

Mr. Grady

Mr. Grady is the owner of the general store. He directs Lily to the Boatwright house.

Sarah Fontanel

Sarah Fontanel is Deborah's mother, Lily's grandmother, and August Boatwright's former boss.

Major Themes

Motherhood

Motherhood is closely tied to love in the novel. Lily's goal throughout the novel is to understand her true mother. She does not understand what the presence of a mother would really be like, but she feels her mother's absence constantly. At some developmental milestones throughout her life, Lily deeply feels her lack of a mother. Though Lily fantasizes about a replacement mother in Rosaleen, she still yearns for the real thing.

Lily leaves Sylvan because T. Ray tells her that her mother, Deborah, left her as a child. She travels to Tiburon in order to learn the truth about her mother. She hopes to find someone who knew something about Deborah in order to answer all of the questions she has. More importantly, however, she is trying to find evidence that T. Ray is wrong and her mother did not leave her. It would be better to find out that she had accidentally killed her mother, for at least this fact would not diminish her perception of her mother's love for her.

Upon settling into her new life in Tiburon, Lily finds motherly love where she did not expect it. The Boatwright sisters and the Daughters of Mary all love her with different styles, and she turns to them with different needs. August, most of all, allows her to open up and cry to her as if she would to a mother.

When Lily learns the truth about her mother's actions, she has mixed feelings of anger, pity, and grief. She is angry after finding that her mother left her after all. She feels sorry that her mother never truly escaped from her life with T. Ray, and she grieves her mother's death.

At the end of the novel, she learns that her mother did love her through a photograph documenting their interaction. She also learns that despite the loss of her mother, she has found the love she sought in her new Tiburon mothers, from Mary, and even from the bees.

Dependence

Interdependence is a basic element of human beings and human society. At many points in the novel, the dependence or interdependence of various characters is expressed through their interactions. The dependent person often becomes the one on whom others depend later.

Lily and Rosaleen often switch between being the stronger woman or the dependent one in their relationship. Though Rosaleen is the older and more typically independent character, she often depends on Lily for leadership and direction. Yet, Lily often depends on Rosaleen for stability, love, and mothering. The two are clearly interdependent, though this aspect of their relationship wanes as they become integrated into the Boatwright home.

May seems to be the most dependent character in the novel due to the great pain that she bears. Yet, after she learns of Zach's arrest, she begins to make independent decisions regarding her future. As an extreme example of this independence, she ends up taking her own life. The Boatwright sisters continue on after May's death, but it becomes apparent that many of the traditions they know and love can be attributed to May.

The bees demonstrate a non-human form of interdependence. At one point in the novel, August shows Lily what happens to the hive when the queen is not present. The bees lay dormant eggs and ultimately sit around without any sort of purpose. Without the queen, the bees are rendered useless; they are extremely dependent on the queen. At the same time, the queen depends on her attendants to take care of the hive.

Lily finds moments of solace when she is working with others. She finds relief from grieving over her mother when she is massaging honey into Mary. She finds comfort in her eight "mothers" at the end of the novel. She accepts her dependence on others as a replacement for her dependence on her mother's memory.

Bees as Models of Human Society

August teaches Lily the important lessons of beekeeping. These lessons reflect good practices of life in general. For instance, she teaches Lily to manage her anger—not to swat the bees, for angry actions are counterproductive with bees. She tells Lily to act as though she knows what she is doing, not to be an idiot. Such lessons as these are tolerably good rules to live by.

When May passes away, August drapes the hives as a sign of respect and mourning. Lily learns the story of the first beekeeper and how his bees came back to life. Bees seem to have an interconnection with death. It seems that all humans have such an interconnection as well, whether or not they want to admit it.

All of the worker bees depend upon the queen's existence, or they do not appropriately function. When one of August's queen bees disappears, she needs to replace it in order to save all of the attendant bees. Similarly, the queen bee depends upon her attendants to keep the hive functioning. The bees' interdependence mirrors the interdependence of humankind.

Lily comments about the precise work that the bees produce. Their work, though instinctive, shows effort and diligence. August argues that bees are smarter than dolphins, and Lily comments about how hard they work. She thinks they work too hard and should take a break. Lily's reflection seems to apply to her feelings about people, those who seem to work too hard and never stop. These "worker bee" types live for their work and create quality work, but they often do not take the time to enjoy life.

Finally, August says that the heat makes the bees act out of sorts. This statement could also be applied to humans. For example, in the hot Tiburon sun, June and Rosaleen are compelled to have a water fight in their front yard. This action, like that of the bees in the heat, is completely incongruent with their characters. In unusual circumstances, people act in unusual ways.

Coping Mechanisms

Throughout the novel, all of the characters are forced to cope with difficulty. They cope with grief, discrimination, abuse, and physical pain. They all use different methods to cope, and no two characters take the same approach.

May takes the most outward approach to coping. Her singing of "Oh Susannah" and leaving the room to go to her wailing wall are clear signals to everyone else that she is disturbed. This is a significant contrast to Lily's efforts at coping, which typically involve her lying down and avoiding her feelings. Ultimately, she takes out her bottled anger in a raging tantrum, destroying the interior.

Zach copes with being jailed by taking a new, somewhat vengeful interest in race relations and civil rights. He almost exclusively discusses topics such as civil rights and the KKK. As for August, she allows her true fire to show after Zach's jailing, exhibiting a new passion in her eyes.

T. Ray coped with Deborah's death by turning to anger and becoming bitter towards Lily. This bitterness becomes apparent at the end of the novel, when T. Ray calls Lily Deborah. Deborah, for her part, coped with her unhappy life with T. Ray by escaping to the Boatwrights' home, even if she had to leave her baby behind to do so.

Transference of Misery

Pain and misery are easily transferred from one person to the next in the novel, where characters pass their sorrow back and forth. This transference and sharing of pain might ease the load borne by one person, but it also expands the reach of the pain.

T. Ray caused Deborah great pain in their marriage, enough that she ran away to the Boatwrights' without Lily. Deborah's pain thus began to lessen, but she died before having much chance to become truly happy. As a result, T. Ray and Lily absorb the pain of Deborah's death. T. Ray takes out his pain on Lily, most vividly at the end of the novel, when he tries to hit Lily and calls her Deborah.

May absorbs everyone's pain. She takes the pain of friends, neighbors, and those she sees in the news. She makes all of this pain her own. She attempts to transfer this pain into her wailing wall. However, she cannot bear the burden and ultimately kills herself. This action transfers pain to the other Boatwright sisters and the Daughters of Mary.

June's first fiancé caused her great pain by leaving her at the altar. In turn, June absorbs that pain and later transfers it to Neil. June refuses to marry Neil because of the pain she felt earlier. It is not until after May's death that June allows herself to be happy by marrying Neil.

Finally, Zach is caused pain by the seeming injustice of a society that would jail three black boys when only one of them is guilty. He expresses his pain by focusing his interests on changing the world and civil rights. Lily absorbs Zach's pain and thus finds herself pained, missing her earlier, much simpler interactions with Zach.

Race Relations

The summer of 1964 in South Carolina comes at just about the boiling point for race relations in American history. The summer of the Civil Rights Act, a summer during which Martin Luther King was advocating thoroughly for equality, was also a summer when much of white America remained disdainful towards blacks. Kidd incorporates race relations into her novel in order to paint an accurate picture of life during this time in the American South.

Rosaleen works as a domestic housekeeper in the Owens' house, a typical role for a working black woman at the time. Lily considers Rosaleen a member of their family despite her lack of biological relation to them. Rosaleen has some fight in her for the sake of equal rights. For example, she attempts to register to vote on the first day that she can. She refuses to take abuse from anyone regardless of skin color. Her fighting attitude ultimately lands her in jail.

Lily's interactions with the Boatwrights and the Daughters of Mary allow her to see some of the lines drawn between white and black. Lily begins to realize her own prejudices about what she believed black people could or could not attain. She also finds that June discriminates against her due to her skin color, something she had never experienced before.

Lily also gets a more clear understanding of society's view of race through her relationship with Zach. Prior to meeting Zach, Lily could not imagine how she could find a black man attractive. Despite Zach's and Lily's love, their society will not accept them as a couple. They vow that someday they will be together, but they understand that right now, interracial dating is strongly taboo.

Zach decides to attend a white high school. Despite all of the challenges that come along with integration, Zach feels that he must be one of the students who take a stand on behalf of a peaceful social revolution. Lily and Clayton Forrest's daughter Becca are outwardly friendly toward Zach at school, which garners them a certain reputation. In spite of those who do not like such friendships, they allow their fondness for Zach to overcome the racism of others.

Ignorance versus Knowledge

Lily spends the beginning of the novel ignorant about her past, about her family, and about a life beyond Sylvan, South Carolina. She is a young girl who believes she can amount to very little, and she has settled into a routine of abuse from T. Ray. Yet, she always hungers for knowledge, wanting to know more about her world, her past, and (most deeply) her mother. The search for knowledge all too often provides knowledge which perhaps had remained hidden for a reason, for this knowledge often brings sorrow.

Lily is basically ignorant about her mother except for what she remembers about the day of her mother's death. T. Ray gradually explains that she had left both T. Ray and Lily, which angers Lily greatly. She goes on a quest to Tiburon in hopes of learning more about her mother. Yet, when she does, she learns the burden associated with such knowledge. She is overcome by emotions including anger, pity, and grief. She is heavy with the knowledge that yes, her mother did leave her, but she also learns that her mother did try to come back for her out of love for her.

May takes in knowledge in a way that is different from her sisters. She absorbs the knowledge and feels the pain associated with troubling events. She feels the pain as if it were her own. Therefore, her sisters try to shield her from the pain associated with Zach's jailing. Yet, when she finds out about it, she is pained that her sisters tried to keep her ignorant of the facts. She is also pained by the situation at hand. She finally kills herself.

Lily is constantly bothered about not knowing what T. Ray has been feeling since she ran away. She feels gnawed by the hope that T. Ray misses her and regrets the awful way that he treated her. Yet, her lack of knowledge drives her to find out the truth about T. Ray's reactions. She calls him and finds that he has felt angry and frustrated. She realizes that he has not missed her and has not felt apologetic, which crushes her hopes and hurts her further.

Zach is fairly laid-back and relaxed until the incident for which he is jailed. After that event, he is awakened by a new knowledge of injustice. This knowledge provides him with a new fire and anger for equality. He thus devotes his time and conversation to civil rights and related issues, even if his new mission pushes Lily away somewhat.

Glossary of Terms

Bee patrol

Bee patrol occurs when the beekeeping staff go to all of the hives in the town, empty the supers, and check on the status of the hives.

Biddy

A biddy is a small chick dyed a color for Easter.

Cooling the hives

Cooling the hives is the process that bees use to protect the hive from intense heat. The bees all beat their wings to fan down the hive interior.

Daughters of Mary

The Daughters of Mary is a group of women made up of Queenie, Violet, Lunelle, Mabelee, Cressie, and the Boatwrights. They worship Our Lady of Chains (Mary) and come together for solidarity.

Draping the hives

Draping the hives is the act of placng a drape over the beehives. This is done in order to signal mourning as well as to keep the bees inside.

Feast of the Assumption

The Feast of the Assumption celebrates the day that Mary died and rose to heaven. It is celebrated on August 15.

Honey gate

The honey gate is a faucet used to drain the honey from large containers.

Honey house

The honey house is the shack behind the Boatwright house that serves as the storage room for all of the beekeeping supplies. Lily and Rosaleen live in the honey house, and when Rosaleen moves into the Boatwright house, Lily occupies the honey house alone.

Manna

Manna is a mix of seeds that the Daughters of Mary eat on ritual occasions.

Mary Day

Mary Day is a two-day celebration commemorating the Assumption of Mary. In the Boatwright house, this celebration involves much cooking, baking, and decorating. The story of Our Lady of Chains is reenacted.

Mary's cake

Mary's cake is a traditional baked good made with honey and eaten on Mary's Day. Those present at the celebration feed each other the cake.

Our Lady of Chains

Our Lady of Chains is an effigy of the Virgin Mary that the Boatwrights own. The statue is large and projects Mary in a position of strength with a fist in the air. Mary is portrayed as a black woman, which is an image the Boatwrights relate to. The story behind the statue is that it broke through the chains. Our Lady of Chains and Mary are often used interchangeably in the novel.

Settling tank

In the settling tank, the honey is heated to about 100 degrees Fahrenheit.

Snuff

Snuff is tobacco that is breathed in through the nose. Rosaleen uses snuff throughout the novel, and Lily at one point steals a can of snuff for her.

Spinner

The spinner is a machine that separates out the good parts of the honey from the bad. August says she wishes such a machine could exist for people.

Supers

Supers are the trays of honeycombs made by the bees. Each tray is sealed by a layer of beeswax. These are what are harvested to create the honey.

Swarm

A swarm occurs when a queen and a group of bees leave the hive to find a new place to live.

Uncapper

The uncapper is a machine that removes the wax from the honeycomb.

Wailing Wall

The Wailing Wall in Jerusalem is the last remaining wall of the Holy Temple. Jews go to this wall to pray, for it is considered the closest accessible location to the Holy Temple. Visitors place their hopes, prayers, and wishes into crevices in the wall. May's wailing wall mirrors that of the wall in Jerusalem. She has built a stone wall outside of the Boatwright house, and she inserts slips of paper on behalf of people in pain.

Watering the bees

Watering the bees involves sprinkling sugar water over the hives when the temperature reaches over 100 degrees. At this temperature, the bees cannot create food for themselves.

Glossary of Terms

Short Summary

Lily Owens begins her adventure with bees in the summer of 1964. She is fourteen years old, and she lives in Sylvan, South Carolina, with her abusive father, T. Ray, and her housekeeper, Rosaleen. Lily's mother died when she was four years old. Her only memory of her mother is from the day she died; Lily recalls that she may have picked up a gun and accidentally killed her mother.

The day the Civil Rights Act is passed, Rosaleen decides that she is going to register to vote. To avoid the monotony on the Owens' peach farm, Lily accompanies Rosaleen. On the way to register, Rosaleen gets harassed by local racist white men. Rosaleen's response is to pour snuff spit all over their shoes, getting herself beaten severely by her accusers and arrested.

T. Ray picks up Lily at the police station, and the two of them get into a fight. T. Ray finally tells Lily that her mother left her, angering Lily enough that she runs away. Lily goes to pick up Rosaleen, and she ultimately has to sneak Rosaleen out of the hospital. The two of them hitchhike to Tiburon, South Carolina. Lily picks this city because she once found her mother's picture of a black Mary with the town etched into the back.

Lily and Rosaleen successfully get a ride to Tiburon and spend a night in the woods. The next day, Lily enters a general store and finds that her mother's black Mary picture matches the labels on jars of Black Madonna Honey. Lily asks the store owner, Mr. Grady, to direct her to where the honey is made. He sends Lily to the Boatwrights' pink house.

Upon reaching the Boatwrights' house, Lily lies about her intentions. She says that she is an orphan with nowhere to stay and is on her way to visit her aunt. She meets the family of three black sisters. August Boatwright invites them to stay as long as they need. May Boatwright carries the weight of the world in her heart, and June Boatwright is not pleased with Lily staying in their house. The women have a group of friends called the Daughters of Mary, and all of them together worship Our Lady of Chains, a black Mary who was able to break the chains that bound her.

In return for her room and board, Lily is required to assist August with the beekeeping. Lily learns how the bee world reflects the human world, and she learns to send love to the bees. She begins to love her life in Tiburon, but she feels awful about keeping her secret from August.

After a week at the Boatwrights', Lily meets Zach, a black boy who works in the bee yard. She instantly is taken by how handsome he is, and she is surprised by her own ability to be attracted to a black boy. The two of them get to know each other and shortly fall in love.

It is about this point that Lily finds May participating in an old habit of Deborah's, making trails of crumbs to lead bugs out of the house. Lily decides to ask May if May ever knew Lily's mother, and May confirms that Deborah lived in the honey house for a while. Lily becomes obsessed with the idea that her mother was in the same place that she is.

On one outing to put honey jars in an office, Zach runs into his friend Jackson and two other boys. They are confronted by a group of white men who are prepared to protest against a white movie star attending a movie with a black woman, as the rumor goes. Jackson throws a bottle at one of the white men, and the four black boys, Zach included, are all put in jail.

The Boatwrights and their friend Attorney Clayton Forrest all do their best to get Zach out of jail. However, they must wait. They visit him, but they have to be patient until Judge Monroe returns to his office. In the meantime, June, August, and Rosaleen resolve not to tell May about Zach's incarceration.

One night, while the family is watching television, May answers the phone and speaks with Zach's mother. This is how May learns that Zach had been jailed. May feels upset that no one told her about the incident before, and she is upset for Zach himself. She decides to partake in her usual ritual to relieve her pain: going out to her "wailing wall." This time, May does not come back. The other women find her dead in the river, having killed herself.

Riddled with grief, the family sits with May's body in the living room in order to prepare for the burial. The Daughters of Mary sit and make jokes about white funerals, and Lily finally feels that she has been accepted as one of them. On the day of May's funeral, Lily recalls the hum of the bees surrounding them.

A few days after the funeral, the Boatwright house celebrates Mary's Day, a two-day commemoration of the Feast of the Assumption. The women bake, decorate, and reenact the story of Our Lady in Chains. After the first night of the Mary Day celebration, Lily decides to come clean with August. She tells August all about her past and how she got to Tiburon. In turn, August tells Lily about her mother's upbringing and tells Lily that Deborah left Lily in Sylvan to come to the Boatwright house. Lily is left with mixed emotions of both anger and pity for her mother.

That night, Lily trashes the honey house out of anger. She breaks jars of honey and throws buckets. She eventually tires herself out and falls asleep. Rosaleen wakes her, and the two of them clean up the honey house. For the second day of Mary's Day, Lily is bitter. It is not until the Daughters participate in the ritual of massaging Our Lady with honey that Lily cheers up. She becomes content working with the women to preserve the statue.

That evening, August comes to the honey house with a box of Lily's mother's belongings. Lily receives a mirror, a brush, and a whale pin that belonged to her mother. Most importantly, August hands Lily a photo of Deborah and Lily smiling at each other. Lily realizes that her mother did love her and cherish her as a mother should. At this point, Lily falls into grief, missing her mother more than ever.

Still in a bit of a funk, Lily does not accompany Rosaleen to register to vote in Tiburon. Instead, she spends the day writing in her notebook. A knock at the door reveals that T. Ray has come to take her back to Sylvan. Lily negotiates, and T. Ray becomes enraged and confused by Deborah's earlier interaction with the Boatwrights. Lily realizes that T. Ray must have loved Deborah deeply, and he must have fallen into depression when she died. It becomes clear that T. Ray does not need Lily around him after all, for she reminds him of Deborah, so he allows her to remain in the care of the Boatwrights.

In the fall, June gets married and Lily starts school. Zach has decided to go to the white school with Lily. Clayton Forrest gives his assurance that Lily and Rosaleen are not getting charged with any crimes back in Sylvan. Lily feels blessed that she is surrounded by the love of her many Tiburon mothers.

Summary and Analysis of Chapters 1 and 2

The book opens in the summer of 1964 with Lily Owens, age fourteen, lying in bed watching bees fly into her room. She recalls her mother's death, which occurred when Lily was four years old. She alludes to some sort of accident and thinks that it was not Lily's fault. In her mother's absence, Lily has lived with her disgruntled father, T. Ray Owens. He is abusive and cold, and Lily does her best to avoid him.

During nights alone in her room, Lily sees swarms of bees entering her room. The threat of being stung scares her, but she finds the sight of so many bees amazing. She runs to wake up T. Ray to show him the swarm, but when they return back to Lily's room, the bees have disappeared, which annoys T. Ray. Despite Lily's insistence that the bees existed, T. Ray does not believe her, so Lily decides to catch the bees to prove it to T. Ray.

Lily flashes back to her only memory of her mother, which was from the day she died, December 3, 1954. Lily remembers that her mother was packing frantically that day, and then T. Ray entered the house. Lily's mother became even more rushed with his presence. When T. Ray entered the room, they began to fight, and Lily was pulled out of the room. Lily's mother then grabbed a gun. T. Ray grabbed the gun away and dropped it on the floor. Lily picked up the gun, and as far as her memory goes, she thinks she shot her mother.

Lily and T. Ray have been living on a peach farm in Sylvan, South Carolina. The kids at Lily's school ridicule her for the giant peach that stands by the gate of the farm, calling it "the Great Fanny." Lily is not a very social girl, and she makes her own clothes. She is disappointed by her looks and her inability to be a girl.

Rosaleen, the Owens' black housekeeper (age unknown), does her best to reassure Lily of her charms. Lily knows that despite her sharp tongue, Rosaleen loves Lily endlessly. Rosaleen stands up for Lily in the face of T. Ray. Rosaleen was born into a large family in McClellanville, South Carolina, but she does not know where any of her siblings are. She married, but she kicked her husband out for cheating on her. Lily dreams of Rosaleen being her real mother.

Lily's mother's name was Deborah, a name that T. Ray refuses to say. Lily has been able to learn very little about her mother. Lily has often missed her mother during specifically feminine moments like buying a bra or getting her first period. Lily does find relics of her mother in her attic: a small bag containing a photo of Deborah, a pair of white gloves, and a small wooden picture of a black Mary with "Tiburon, S.C." scratched into the back. Lily has kept her mother's belongings buried in the backyard. Lily makes a goal of traveling to Tiburon one day, for she wants to go everywhere her mother had ever been.

Spending afternoons selling peaches for T. Ray from a roadside stand, Lily is consistently bored, but she is not allowed to bring books to entertain her. Lily loves reading, and one of her teachers, Mrs. Henry, provides insight into how bright Lily's future could be. Mrs. Henry encourages Lily to consider a profession as a writer or a professor. Lily accepts that her future could lead to writing, which she loves. Lily writes whenever she gets the chance. T. Ray mocks her for her endeavors, but Lily spends her time in the peach stand writing poetry.

The day before Lily starts first grade, T. Ray confronts Lily about what happened to Deborah. He says she was cleaning out the closet, and T. Ray is shocked when Lily confesses that she remembers. T. Ray says that after she picked up the gun, it just went off, killing her mother. He adds that Lily did not mean to do it, so now she knows what happened.

The nation has begun to obsess over Khrushchev and the possibility of being bombed by the Soviet Union. Lily's school begins bomb drills. Around the same time, President Johnson signs the Civil Rights Act into law, and Rosaleen is thrilled. Lily is worried, however, that the law might cause an uproar among the white community.

Lily's birthday is approaching, and she is thinking about how to delicately approach the topic with T. Ray. Every year, she hopes that T. Ray will acknowledge her birthday with a special gift—perhaps a silver charm bracelet—but he never does. When Lily mentions the bracelet, she is ignored.

That night, Lily goes to the backyard to dig up her mother's belongings, and she falls asleep in the orchard. She is awakened by T. Ray running through the trees looking for her. He accuses her of being out in the backyard with someone, and he punishes her with kneeling on grits, a painful punishment she has been enduring since she was six. She is left with small welts all over her knees. Up until that point, Lily thought that maybe T. Ray loved her a bit, but afterwards she feels convinced that he does not.

Rosaleen tells Lily that she will be registering to vote on the Fourth of July. Lily begs Rosaleen to take her along. Lily gets permission from T. Ray under the pretense that she is going to town to buy female sanitary supplies, a topic that T. Ray avoids.

That night, Lily attempts to let her bees go. She unscrews the lid of the jar which held them, but the bees do not move. They are still there the next morning, when Rosaleen walks into Lily's bedroom with a birthday cake. They begin their long walk to town, and the two of them stop to rest in the church.

The church minister walks in to find Lily and Rosaleen, and he shows an obvious look of disapproval that Lily is accompanied by a black woman. The minister makes small talk and wishes Lily a happy birthday. Rosaleen asks if they could borrow church fans for Lily's birthday, but the minister refuses. As Lily and Rosaleen leave the church, Rosaleen steals the fans.

Once the two are in town in Sylvan, several men call out to Rosaleen in an insulting and derogatory way. Rosaleen says that she is registering to vote, but the men continue to mock her. After continued harassment, Rosaleen decides to fight back, pouring the snuff spit she had collected all over the shoes of the men. They demand that Rosaleen apologize and clean their shoes, but she refuses. The men call the police and then beat Rosaleen. When the police arrive, Rosaleen is arrested, and the officer tells Lily they will call T. Ray for her.

The three men who assaulted Rosaleen follow them to the police station. When they get out of the car, Rosaleen is handcuffed and the men continue to beat her. Rosaleen suffers a heavy blow to the head. The men threaten to continue, but Officer Gaston takes Rosaleen and Lily into the jailhouse out of harm's way. After half an hour, T. Ray comes to pick Lily up, but Rosaleen has to stay in jail.

Lily begs T. Ray to get Rosaleen out of jail, but he explains that Rosaleen chose to dump spit all over the most racist man in town. Upon returning home, T. Ray tells Lily not to think about leaving the house, and Lily responds that he does not scare her. She and T. Ray get into a fight ending with T. Ray attempting to punch Lily in the face. Lily claims that her mother would have kept her safe, but T. Ray replies that Deborah did not care about Lily and that in fact she intentionally had left Lily behind. Lily sinks, and her mind rattles around her father's statement. She decides to leave T. Ray's house and get Rosaleen out of jail.

She takes $38, some clothing, toiletries, and her mother's belongings. She writes T. Ray a note and leaves with T. Ray running after her. Lily ponders where she will go after she meets Rosaleen, and she concludes that she must go to Tiburon. At the station, Officer Gaston informs Lily that Rosaleen is at the hospital because she had "fallen and hit her head." Lily heads to the hospital, despite warnings from Officer Gaston that she will not be permitted to see Rosaleen.

Lily sneaks by the officer stationed at the hospital and finds Rosaleen. Her head is bandaged heavily, and she tells Lily that the police allowed the men who had harassed Rosaleen to beat her up. Rosaleen still refused to apologize to them.

Despite Rosaleen's protests, Lily devises a plan to get Rosaleen out of the hospital. Lily calls the hospital pretending to be the jailer's wife with instructions that the officer guarding Rosaleen must go back to the station. Once the officer leaves the hospital, Rosaleen and Lily walk out. They begin thumbing for a ride. Eventually a black man selling melons picks them up and agrees to drop them three miles from Tiburon.

Once they get out of the car, Lily explains that they have traveled to Tiburon due to Lily's hope that she would find someone who knew her mother. She tells Rosaleen what T. Ray said about Deborah leaving Lily. Lily hopes Rosaleen can provide contradictory information, but Rosaleen replies that she only saw Deborah from a distance and noticed that she always seemed sad. This angers Lily, and she and Rosaleen argue before going to bed in a forest.

When Lily awakens in the night, she cannot find Rosaleen, so she panics. She finds Rosaleen bathing in the river and then apologizes for their fight. Rosaleen does the same. Lily is still consumed by thoughts of her mother.

Analysis

At the beginning of the book, the parallels between humans and bees begin. The first link is established between bees and Lily's mother, Deborah. The name "Deborah" is a translation from the Hebrew for "bee." In addition, Lily interprets the swarms of bees that enter her room to be signs that come directly from her mother. Along with the bees come words of advice and comfort from an unknown voice.

Lily's character is developed in these chapters as a child who has suffered a rough past. She not only has lived through the traumatic event of her mother's death, but she also feels tremendous guilt for causing her death. She remembers enough to know that she bears some responsibility, although she has never understood why her mother had been gone and was packing. Meanwhile, her father, T. Ray, is abusive and cold. These aspects of her family life help the reader understand why Lily is so sad and a bit peculiar. She expects disappointment, and she has come to accept that she will not grow up to become much. It is not until her teacher, Mrs. Henry, intervenes and supports her that she starts to see herself as having a productive future.

Kidd paints amazing descriptions of the setting surrounding Lily in South Carolina. She uses specific metaphors in addition to the symbol of the bees when she compares lightning to "soft golden licks across the sky." She also uses personification, writing that the "darkness pulls the moon to the top of the sky." In addition, she interweaves nature imagery with emotions to paint the scene, explaining, for instance, that "sunset is the saddest light there is."

The use of Lily's memory serves two purposes. First of all, since Lily can remember aspects of her mother's death, she can provide most the information in the first person. No one else is needed to tell Lily's story. The way that Lily retells the story allows the reader to gain the perspective of a sad and confused child in the midst of chaos.

Second, Lily's blurred memory creates holes that Lily herself will work to fill in. Someone else needs to tell her mother's story, and Lily will try to do so by journeying into her mother's past and going everywhere her mother has been. T. Ray abuses his position as Lily's father when he apparently lies, telling Lily that her mother was leaving in part to abandon her. This is not a story that fits Lily's understanding of motherhood and love, so she becomes disturbed enough to leave her cold father behind and seek a more believable truth.

The theme of race relations is established immediately in this first section of the book. Lines are drawn between black and white across all settings: in the home, in church, in town, regarding crime and justice, and even in art and religion, as depicted by the black Mary picture among Deborah's belongings. South Carolina in 1964 is certainly a hotbed of racial tension. Although the Civil Rights Act is in force, the citizens themselves are slow to accept the essential equality of people of different races. Rosaleen is ready to take up her rights, however, and Lily seems to have no problem whatsoever of appreciating Rosaleen on the basis of who she is—in some ways, the mother Lily has not had.

The relationships that matter, for them, are guided more by gender than by race. That is, the two are bonding as females against people like the racist men and T. Ray. Although Lily is somewhat quick to get into fights, she has had enough of T. Ray while she actively seeks out Rosaleen to make up after their fight.

Summary and Analysis of Chapters 3 and 4

Waking up in the woods that morning, Lily considers this day to be the first day of her new life. She watches Rosaleen sleep and tries to determine why her mother would have a picture of black Mary. When Rosaleen wakes up, she complains of the pain she suffered during her beating the night before. As they walk toward Tiburon, they discuss the next steps in their plan. Lily decides that she needs a sign. Her plan is to take nine steps and look up. Her eyes land on a crop duster, which provides little assistance.

After walking in the sweltering heat, Rosaleen and Lily find a general store. Lily goes in, buys some food, and steals snuff for Rosaleen. Most importantly, Lily sees a picture matching her mother's black Mary on jars of honey labeled "Black Madonna Honey." When Lily asks about the picture, the storeowner explains that the owner of the honey company is a black woman, August Boatwright, who lives in the bright pink house. Lily tells Rosaleen, and Rosaleen worries that Lily is getting her hopes up.

On the way to finding August's house, Lily buys a newspaper in order to see if she and Rosaleen are listed as wanted. Lily feels relief after finding no reference to their escape in the entire paper.

Upon reaching the pink house, Lily sees the swarms of bees and beekeeping equipment surrounding the house. Lily and Rosaleen stand nervously in front of the house. After Lily finally musters the courage to knock on the door, May and June Boatwright answer. Lily pretends that she is visiting in search of honey. May and June get August, who impresses Lily as "a mix of mighty and humble all in one." Lily gets the impression from August that she already knows everything about her.

Lily now tells August that she and Rosaleen ran away from home and had nowhere to go. August offers that Rosaleen and Lily may stay at the Boatwright house until they find a place to live. June seems to protest the arrangement, but August ignores her. Lily asks why all of the Boatwright sisters are named after months. May explains that their mother loved the spring and summer—and there is a fourth Boatwright sister, April, who died when they were young. May's response to this discussion is to leave the room, singing "Oh Susannah."

Lily tells the Boatwrights that both of her parents have died and that she was left without any family. She says that Rosaleen was the family housekeeper and that the two of them are on their way to Virginia to stay with Lily's aunt. August replies that she is also from Virginia, and she discusses the terms of Lily's and Rosaleen's stay. Rosaleen will help May in the house, and Lily will assist with the beekeeping. Lily is sure that August can see right through her lies.

August sets up the honey house so that Lily and Rosaleen can sleep inside. August tells Lily that she can start work the next morning and shows her the beekeeping equipment. Lily begins to note her own whiteness and her own prejudices. She instructs Rosaleen not to mention the black Mary picture. Rosaleen reassures her that she can do whatever she chooses with her own secret.

Lily learns that August's grandfather left her the land that she uses to keep the bees. She also discovers what is later revealed as May's "wailing wall," a stone wall with small notes stuck inside it. Lily thinks that she wants nothing to change. She would be content for life always to remain like this.

Analysis

Lily is depicted as a very thoughtful and introspective girl throughout the novel, and in this section her depth of thought is shown through her creation and interpretation of metaphors in the world around her. For example, when Lily takes nine steps and looks up for a sign, she is confused about which part of the scene above her represents her. She could either be the rescued plants, the murdered bugs, or the airplane.

Note that Kidd uses alliteration frequently, most often to set scenes. For example, when describing the setting in Tiburon, she explains that "perspiration puddles" and "collarbones came together." Sweat "dripped down." Using such hard consonants in succession adds to the feeling of heaviness and harshness of the environment surrounding Rosaleen and Lily.

At the Boatwright house, Lily begins to learn that August too sees a symbol in bees; beekeeping and bee society represent human life and human society. The first example of this metaphor occurs when August introduces Lily to the spinner, which separates the good and bad parts of the honey. August states that she wishes the spinner could be used on people, separating the good from the bad.

Rosaleen instantly changes when she reaches the Boatwrights'. The past few days for Rosaleen have been filled with horror and pain, and Lily commented that her face had lost its shine. However, when she first crosses the yard to the honey house, walking under the rain, Lily begins to see Rosaleen's old liveliness come back to her. Rosaleen is now in an environment primarily of black females, quite different from the one where she was beaten up by white men on her way to exercise her civil rights.

Lily begins to question her own notions about race after she meets the Boatwright sisters. She becomes very aware of her whiteness when she is surrounded by black women. She also understands now that she has held prejudices concerning the level of intelligence of a black person versus that of a white person. In particular, Lily can sense that August can see through her lies and that August knows much more than she is revealing. Such moments of understanding allow Lily to recognize her prejudice, and later she will be able to cast it aside.

Lily has something powerfully in common with the sisters; they all have lost their mothers. The death of family members does not seem to weigh heavily on the daily lives of the sisters, except for May, who maintains a "wailing wall." Lily and her father, however, have never recovered from the accidental death of Lily's mother. Lily is likely to learn some things about coping with loss from her time with the Boatwrights.

Summary and Analysis of Chapters 5 and 6

Lily finds that living with the Boatwrights provides an oasis apart from the rest of her life. August gives Rosaleen new clothes, and Rosaleen insists that she will repay her for them. Lily notices that May again sings "Oh Susannah" and leaves the room. May teaches Lily the honey song. Everything is honey and beeswax. The women eat honey at every meal, and beeswax cures every ailment.

May and Rosaleen become fast friends. Rosaleen discovers that May regularly begins to sing "Oh Susannah" in response to unpleasant subjects. The humming often leads to tears, and her only comfort during these episodes is to visit her stone wall outside. May loves all living things, and she refuses to harm even the smallest spiders. May loves bruise-free bananas almost as much as honey, but she disposes of the flawed fruit. Rosaleen does her best to put the bruised bananas to use through various banana recipes, but at last August convinces her to just throw them away.

June is a little more difficult to understand. She was a teacher, and she now plays the cello for dying people. Lily overhears June insisting to August that Lily and Rosaleen were lying about their backgrounds. August agrees, but she insists that the Boatwrights can offer help. June also is discontent with Lily staying in their house because she is white. At the end of the night, while going to the bathroom, Lily has a revelation: her urine is no different from June's.

In the evenings, the women watch the news. They watch the unfolding of the events of the Civil Rights Movement, and Lily feels even more self-conscious about her whiteness. May often skips the news, often forced into her ritual of "Oh Susannah" and crying. After the news, the women pray to a statue of black Mary which they call "Our Lady of Chains." August explains that the sisters have taken the Catholicism of their mother and added their own twist.

August assures Lily that if Lily asks for Mary's help, she will provide it. August tells Lily a story about a runaway nun who received the help of Mary. Lily asks Mary for assurance that she will never have to return home and that the police will not apprehend her and Rosaleen.

Lily begins receiving lessons from August about "bee etiquette," which August again equates to the human world. Lily learns lessons about not being an idiot and sending out love. August keeps her bees in farmers' yards all over Tiburon. Checking on these hives is called "Bee Patrol." Lily wants August to want to love her and keep her forever.

August and Lily discuss May's wall. May built the wall out of stones from the river. She has spent ten years building it. August explains that May is very susceptible to feeling the pain of others. She treats the pain as her own. Lily wondered what it would be like if someone shared the pain she had. August tells Lily that May had a twin sister April, and May would suffer the symptoms of April's injuries and sickness. When April died as a young child, May began to absorb the pain of the world. April had suffered from terrible depression as a child, and at age fifteen she killed herself. June and August had decided to start the wailing wall to assist May with her pain. May writes down the names of people in pain or events that caused pain, and she puts the notes in the wall.

Lily is constantly swelling in feelings. She hopes that T. Ray feels sorry for being a poor father. She misses her mother, and she wonders about the details of Deborah's life.

Rosaleen begins to express jealousy that Lily has been spending most of her time with August. Rosaleen warns Lily about delving too deeply into her mother's past in order to protect herself. Lily puts a piece of paper with her mother's name on it into May's wailing wall.

At the beginning of Chapter Six, Lily meets Neil for the first time. Upon meeting Lily, Neil asks a series of questions that Lily feels she will not be able to avoid, such as where she is from, how long she is staying, and so on. Neil is in love with June and has continually asked her to marry him. June keeps refusing; she had been engaged before, but her fiancé never showed up to the wedding. When the topic is brought up in front of May, she begins to sing "Oh Susannah" and has to leave for the wailing wall.

On Sundays, the Daughters of Mary group meets for prayer services in the Boatwright house. The Daughters of Mary are mostly women: the Boatwright sisters, Queenie, Violet, Lunelle, Mabelee, Cressie, and Sugar Girl. The group also includes one man, Otis Hill. At these events, June plays the cello and the group recites Hail Marys.

At Lily's first meeting of the Daughters, August retells the story of Our Lady of Chains. The story involves a slave, Obadiah, finding a wooden figure of Mary. Obadiah retrieves the statue, and he hears the statue reassure him that she will take care of him. He brings the statue to the prayer house, and another slave named Pearl explains that the statue is the mother of Jesus. The people celebrate the statue and find strength from touching her heart. Soon, the master discovers the statue and chains it to a barn. Soon, however, the statue is found to have broken the chains.

After the story, the Daughters begin dancing, and then each of them slowly walks up to the statue of Mary to touch her heart. Lily is compelled to do the same, so she rises and walks toward Mary to touch her heart. As she does so, June stops playing the cello, and Lily realizes that she is not included in the ritual. August scolds June for her inhospitality, and Lily faints.

Lily wakes up in August's room after the meeting of the Daughters. Everyone attributes Lily's fainting to the heat of the day. That night, the Boatwright sisters, Lily, and Rosaleen all watch Walter Cronkite tell the country that the United States will be sending a man to the moon. August gets upset by this announcement, and she tells Lily that the mystery of the moon is ending. At the end of the night, Lily resolves that she will touch Mary's heart and that she will show August her mother's picture of black Mary.

Analysis

Lily becomes inculcated with the Boatwrights' obsession for bee products. She learns songs about bees and honey, she eats honey at every meal, and she uses honey to clean herself. Lily instantly realizes such physical differences in her new honey-filled life. There seems to be parallelism between what honey does for Lily's body and what beekeeping does for Lily's soul. Lily's confidence grows due to her skill in beekeeping, and she is happy with her new life in Tiburon.

Lily continues to learn how the bee yard is a symbol for the world at large. When Lily begins beekeeping, she learns rules of the yard and ultimately of the world. Lily also learns lessons like not to be afraid, not to be an idiot, not to express her anger, and to act like she knows what she is doing. Most importantly, Lily is told to send out love.

May's ritual reaction to unpleasant situations, singing "Oh Susannah" and going out to the wailing wall, is a stark contradiction to Lily's tactic for dealing with unpleasantness. While May has an outward reaction, Lily has been avoiding uncomfortable situations, such as ignoring interaction with June. These are two examples of the different coping mechanisms that are exhibited by characters throughout the novel. June's anti-white racism might be June's own way of coping with loss or with the anti-black racism she has experienced herself.

Lily begins to see race relations in a new light. When she interacts with white people now, she is doing so as a white resident in a black home. She finds that people of the same race do their best to connect their families and hometowns, in order to determine if they are interconnected. Lily has found that black people rarely ask her about her background, presumably because they believe that there will be no way for their paths to connect. The irony here, however, is that Lily has deep connections to the Boatwrights through Lily's mother, whose experience directly led Lily to find the bee company and its owners.

The idea of statues coming to life has a long history in literature. Here, the story of Our Lady of Chains is a metaphor for the success of black women in America and specifically for the Boatwrights. Just as Mary was once bound, the Boatwright sisters were forced into work in domestic positions despite their college educations. Yet, once they inherited the bee farm, they were unbound, free to make significant money and successful lives for themselves. In addition, the Boatwrights, like black Mary, send their love and care to their friends within the community. The mythology of black Mary, Our Lady of Chains, seems like the main twist on the Catholicism of the sisters' mother. (In this context, one should remember Kidd's own spiritual journey, not neatly fitting any traditional religion.)

Gender is again brought into relief during the meeting of the Daughters of Mary, for all the members save one are women. Otis Hill is the one man among the women. In this way he is thus a parallel to Lily, the one white person among the Boatwrights. For June, gender is less of a problem than race; Lily is not supposed to be one of the Daughters. Fortunately, June is the exception, and August reasserts her family's hospitality toward Lily.

Summary and Analysis of Chapters 7 and 8

On Monday morning, Lily remembers that today is Zachary Taylor's first day back at work. Zach assists August with the beekeeping, but he has been absent so far during Lily's stay at the Boatwrights'. Lily is unhappy about the prospect of sharing August further. Lily has heard from August that Zach is a straight-A student and a football player. His father left him when he was small, and his mother is a lunch-lady in a school. When Zach arrives, he is surprised that Lily is white, and Lily is surprised that she finds Zach to be handsome. After speaking to Zach for a few minutes, Lily realizes that they will become friends.

They work together in the honey house with August. Lily loves her days, but she hates having to eat dinner with June. Their mutual resentment causes them to ignore each other for most of the meal. After dinner one night, August says that Lily may touch Mary's heart, but Lily refuses because of June's presence. Lily's favorite meal is lunch, which she shares with Zach under the shade of the trees. Lily and Zach confess to each other that they both are unsure about their futures, Lily because she is an orphan, and Zach because he is black. Zach tells Lily that he wants to be a lawyer, and Lily says she has never heard of a black lawyer. Zach tells Lily, "You gotta imagine what's never been."

Rosaleen asks Lily about her long-term intentions with the Boatwrights, considering that they have been living with the Boatwrights for two weeks. June has also begun to call attention to the length of their stay. August reassures them that no one wants them to leave until they are ready to do so. August also tells Lily that Lily can confide in her. Despite her desire to come clean with August, Lily keeps her secret and cries privately.

Neil spends evenings at the house, and Lily eavesdrops. One day, June tells Neil that she cannot marry him. Neil replies that he cannot wait forever, and he leaves.

Lily and Zach are going to spend one morning harvesting honey at a farmhouse in the country. Lily dreams of being physically close with Zach, though her fantasies are not particularly sexual. Zach tells Lily about Attorney Clayton Forrest, who has discussed his law practice with Zach. Lily has been fascinated by the fact that she has become attracted to Zach; earlier she did not think it was possible to be attracted to such a man. The two of them get out of the truck and start the harvesting. Zach puts honey on his finger for Lily to taste. Lily wants Zach to kiss her, and she knows he wants to, but they just continue harvesting the honey.

Zach teaches Lily about a famous Tiburon resident, Willifred Marchant. Willifred has won Pulitzer Prizes for his books about trees in South Carolina. Tiburon celebrates Willifred one day each year. Lily accuses Zach of not believing that she will be successful as a writer, and she begins to cry. Zach pulls her close to him to comfort her. Lily realizes that she is actually crying for Zach, but Zach assumes she is crying because of his supposed lack of confidence in her writing ability.

Rosaleen decides to move into May's room because May gets scared during the night. Lily is annoyed with the decision, but Rosaleen reassures her that she will be beside Lily when she needs to face reality. In following Rosaleen into the pink house, Lily notices that August is reading *Jane Eyre*. When Lily asks what the book is about, August explains that it is about a girl who is lost and sad. Lily takes this as a sign that August knows who she is. The feeling eventually passes.

June and Neil begin to fight outside of the house, and Neil soon leaves while June threatens that if Neil leaves now, he should never come back. Neil gets in the car, and June responds by throwing tomatoes at him. May once again writes their names on a slip of paper, and she puts it into her wall.

Zach and Lily spend the rest of the day processing the honeycombs they harvested. Lily is amazed about how consumed she has felt by her love for Zach. She spends the night alone in the honey house for the first time and daydreams of Zach. She begins to explore her body, and she realizes her development into a woman. Her hunger for Zach is soon replaced, however, by a different sort of hunger for her mother.

Two days later, Zach gives Lily a notebook as a present. He encourages her to start writing in it. Lily realizes that Zach is the best friend she will ever have. Lily hugs him, and Zach confesses that he likes her more than any girl he has ever met—but that he cannot pursue his feelings because of the racial divide between them. Both Lily and Zach express how sorry they are about the situation.

August and Lily spend a day pasting labels onto honey jars. August explains that each of the Boatwright sisters has her own special month corresponding to her name. During their special months as children, the girls were allowed to stay up late and avoid their chores. Lily admires the labels, and she tells August that she had never considered a black Mary before. August explains that there are black Mary paintings all over Europe. Lily confesses her love for the picture, and August asks what else she loves. Lily discusses her love for Rosaleen, writing, the color blue, and Coca-Cola with peanuts in it. August tells Lily that she also loves the color blue and Coca-Cola with peanuts.

Lily asks how the Boatwrights gained possession of the Our Lady statue. August replies that it has always been in her family. She adds that Mary's spirit is everywhere. As August retells her family history, it occurs to Lily that August misses her mother, too. Lily learns that while August's mother did not keep bees, August's grandmother did. Lily asks August about all of the details of her life. August studied at a black college in Maryland and then worked as a housekeeper. August confesses that she has decided against marrying, though she is not against marriage in general. She tells Lily that she has been in love, but she loves her freedom more.

While on bee patrol, Lily learns that May picked the bright pink color for the house. August explains that some things just do not matter that much, and the pink color lifted May's spirits, so it was worth it even though the house looked funny. August also tells Lily that bees have a secret life that people cannot understand, and Lily likes the idea that they have a secret life like she does. During the harvest, the bees flood around Lily, and she loses herself in thought about her mother. Lily is soon shaken back to alertness by August, who announces that she and Lily must speak about Lily's background.

May and Rosaleen make a celebratory lunch of pork chops and okra to commemorate the fact that May has not been out to her wall in five days. Zach tells the group that a rumor is spreading through town that movie star Jack Palance will be visiting the town and plans to take a black woman to the movies with him. The town is buzzing about staging protests outside of the theater. Lily realizes how much importance people put on skin color, and she considers that the world would be better off if skin color differences did not exist.

Zach leaves lunch to go to Clayton Forrest's office to drop off honey, and Lily volunteers to go with him—both to spend time with Zach and to see a real lawyer's office. Lacy, Forrest's secretary, seems confused to hear that Lily is staying in the Boatwrights' house. Lily introduces herself to Clayton with the false story she has been using all along. Clayton and Zach leave the room, and Lily decides to make a collect call to T. Ray, hoping that he will feel remorseful about the way he treated her. T. Ray's reaction to hearing Lily's voice, however, is one of anger and verbal abuse. Lily decides to ask T. Ray if he knows her favorite color. T. Ray responds instead with a threat to "tear your behind to pieces." Lily lowers the phone and forces herself not to cry. Zach returns with a book of cases. Clayton begins asking more about Lily's background, but she uses female trouble as an excuse to leave the office.

That night, Lily writes a letter to T. Ray explaining her disdain for him. She writes an acrostic about how much of a horrible father he is. She then tears up the letter. She goes into the pink house to use the bathroom and then decides to pray to Mary. She asks to know what to do and for help so that Rosaleen can escape her criminal charges. She touches Mary's heart and proclaims that Mary was her mother.

Analysis

As Lily grows in fondness for Zach, and her concept of the divisions between races is more seriously questioned. She finds him attractive, and she does not know what to do about her feelings. The reader can see Lily being characterized more as a young woman than as a child in this relationship. Lily begins to flirt, and she becomes fascinated with Zach's tiny details. For his part, Zach understands race relations in his town well enough to know that he is better off not trying to start a relationship with a young white woman.

August uses stories to symbolize what is taking place in Lily's life. Prior to this section, August told the story of Beatrix, the runaway nun. In Chapter Seven, August is reading *Jane Eyre*. She tells Lily that she has just begun reading, but at the moment the girl is sad and lost, obviously mirroring Lily's feelings. Lily feels as though August is sending her a message that she knows Lily's past. Lily has gotten this feeling a few times before, but again she allows the feeling to pass. August has been waiting patiently for Lily to tell the truth.

June's character is developed more with the introduction of her relationship with Neil. Typically the least vibrant of the Boatwright sisters, June finally allows her emotions to pour out when she throws tomatoes at Neil's car. Her caution about marriage is based on a prior disappointment, but the reader is forced to wonder if June will ever allow herself to get over the past and allow herself to be happy. Her coping mechanism has made her cut herself off from the chance of a marriage because of the chance of a second major rejection. This condition parallels Lily's inability to hurdle her past obstacles (her dead mother and her cold, mean father) in order to reach happiness.

August tries to reach Lily again when she tells Lily that bees have a secret life. This reference, obviously invoking the book's title, serves several purposes. First of all, the secret life of the bees symbolizes both Lily's secret life and the secret life of her mother, Deborah. Notably, May has some kind of secret life that her sisters do their best to negotiate, allowing May to have her wall and the pink paint on the house. In addition, by mentioning the secret life of the bees, August again hints to Lily that she understands that Lily has a secret. Just as the bees are allowed to keep their secrets, August, suggests, August is giving Lily her support even if she wants to keep her secret for a little while longer. Eventually, though, it will be time to come clean.

The queen bee is considered by August to be "the mother of thousands." Lily, on the search for a mother figure, seems to be drawn to potential mothers, including the queen bees. Lily feels a tremendous amount of love from the bees that she keeps. She ultimately finds a mother symbol in Mary. That this is a black Mary is no problem (remember that Lily has realized that everyone's urine is the same color—a strange variation on the common theme that everyone's blood is the same color—so it is notable that Lily turns to this Mary after entering the house to go to the bathroom). Lily accepts Mary as a mother as well as, in the Catholic tradition, the spiritual mother of millions of Christians. Both the queen bee and Mary symbolize the mother that Lily has never really known.

It is interesting that Lily chooses to write T. Ray a letter after their failed phone conversation. Being at the lawyer's office probably gives her a stronger sense that she is again on a path to success, so this is a good time for her to start resolving the issues that have weighed her down in the past. Unfortunately, T. Ray has not changed, but Lily has. She feels comfortable enough with her power of written expression to write down how she feels about him. When she rips up the letter, she is not signaling dissatisfaction with her expressive ability so much as realizing that the letter was her way of coping with the bad conversation—writing the letter for her own sake.

Summary and Analysis of Chapters 9 and 10

The heat in Tiburon becomes scorching, near 100 degrees. August, Lily, and Zach provide the bees with sugar water because it is too hot for them to get food otherwise. While putting a lid back on a hive box, Lily gets stung on her wrist. She assures August that she was sending the bees love, but August replies that the heat makes bees act a bit crazy. August adds that the sting is part of her initiation as a true beekeeper. Lily asks if she has a possible future in beekeeping, and August replies that a person's skill in an activity is not as important as one's love for it.

At lunchtime, Rosaleen and May run fully clothed through the water sprinkler, and August and Lily soon join in the fun, dancing around in the water. Eventually, June comes out to the porch, and Lily sprays her with the hose. At first, June reacts angrily, but then she and Lily start laughing wildly together. June hugs Lily, and they finally make their peace.

One extremely hot day, all of the women take a break and go to bed. Lily lies in the honey house and thinks about telling Rosaleen about her call to T. Ray. Despite her attempts not to think of her mother, Lily does so. Lily puts on her mother's gloves, and she realizes how tight they feel. She realizes that soon she will outgrow them.

Lily escapes her thoughts by going into the pink house for a drink. She finds May making trails of graham crackers and marshmallows to lead bugs out of the house. Lily recalls that T. Ray had mentioned that Lily's mother used to do the same thing. Lily asks May if she remembers a Deborah Fontanel, and May says yes, Deborah stayed out in the honey house for a while. Lily feels light-headed and goes out to the honey house. Lily becomes obsessed with the idea that her mother walked in the very same room in which she stood. Lily eventually falls asleep.

For the next few days, Lily is frazzled and jumpy. The Boatwright women ask what is wrong, but she lies and says that nothing is bothering her. Lily considers discussing her mother with August, but she will not bring herself to have the conversation. That Friday, however, Lily finally prepares to speak to August, putting her mother's black Mary picture in her pocket. Lily is intercepted, however, by Zach, who asks her to join him to run an errand in town.

In town, Zach and Lily see white men preparing to protest against Jack Palance's appearance with a black woman. Zach meets up with a few of his friends. One of them, Jackson, taunts the white men, and one of the white men approaches Jackson with a shovel in a threatening manner. Jackson responds by throwing a cola bottle at the man, which cuts open the white man's nose. The man does not realize which of the boys threw the bottle, and none of them admits to the act. Lily hopes that Zach will point out Jackson, but Zach stands alongside his friends. All four boys are eventually handcuffed and taken away by police. Lily sits frozen in Zach's truck for a while until she decides to walk back to the Boatwright house.

When Lily returns home, August, June, and Rosaleen already know what happened, and Clayton Forrest is at the house. Clayton announces that Judge Monroe is out of town, so there is no chance for Zach to get out of jail for five days. Clayton has seen Zach in jail, and he seems ok. Lily sees the fire in August's eyes about the incident. Clayton reassures them all that he will do his best to get Zach out. Everyone agrees not to tell May about the situation, determining that it would be too much for her. Lily recalls that she saw May that afternoon building onto her wall.

August and Lily go to visit Zach in the local jail. Lily sees him and wants to touch him, but she does not. Lily had prepared some words to say to Zach, but she forgets all of them. She cannot say anything at all. Zach asks Lily if she has been writing in her notebook, and Lily assures him that she will write all of this down for him. August speaks with Zach about the bee business.

The Boatwrights avoid discussing Zach, and one evening they decide to watch Ed Sullivan on television to stop moping. The phone rings, and May answers and talks to Zach's mother. She announces to the group that she now knows that Zach has been in jail, and she is upset that no one had told her. May's eyes gloss over, and she begins to ignore everyone else. May assures everyone that she will be fine, but she goes out to the wall. August offers to accompany her, but May insists that she must go alone.

After twenty minutes, May has not returned, so everyone goes out to find her. They search the wall and call her name in vain. August instructs June to call the police, pray to Mary, and then return. August and Lily begin to walk the river. Lily recites Hail Marys in her head and unintentionally aloud as they look for May. They find May's flashlight on the ground, and soon they find May's body in the river with a stone on top of her. August does her best to revive her sister, but she soon announces that May is dead.

To Lily's surprise, June and August do react not in horror but with "heartbroken acceptance." Rosaleen does not cry, but her chin shakes. Lily hears a pocket of air get released from May's mouth, and she is overcome with nausea. She vomits. She feels as though her dream world is slipping away.

The policemen ask August and June a series of questions about May, but they ask Lily about her own background. Lily sticks to her false story about being an orphan. The policeman seems concerned about Lily staying in the Boatwright house. The policeman advises Lily to move in with her aunt as soon as possible, because she is lowering herself by living with a black family. For her part, Rosaleen makes up the relationship she has with August, saying that she is her husband's first cousin.

Lily reenters the house and begins to cry. Rosaleen asks Lily to share May's room with her. Lily sleeps in Rosaleen's old bed, and Rosaleen now sleeps in May's bed.

Lily dreams about Zach. She wakes with a start, and then the events of the night come flooding back to her. Upon washing her face in the bathroom, Lily notices the socks that May had put on the bathtub's feet. She decides she never wants to forget this side of May. Lily also determines that May's blend of love and pain has ultimately consumed her life.

After an autopsy, the police officially rule May's death a suicide. August explains to Lily that they will sit with May's body until she is buried, and May's coffin is brought into the living room. They hold a vigil to say goodbyes to May and to allow May to understand that those she leaves behind accept that she is moving on. June plays the cello, and Lily looks at May's body. Lily realizes that only six days have passed since she learned that her mother once stayed with the Boatwrights, though it feels like six months. Lily feels an impulse to come clean with August at that moment, but she determines that it is not fair to add this material to August's burden at this time. Lily says goodbye to May internally, but before she leaves the coffin, she rearranges May to look as if she is pondering the future.

Later that morning, Zach finally returns to the Boatwright house. He hugs Lily, but Lily feels that something has disappeared from his face. A witness at the scene of the bottle-throwing incident was able to clear Zach of all charges. Clayton sends his condolences, and Lily watches the interaction between August and Rosaleen. Lily realizes that August loves Rosaleen. Zach considers May's death to be entirely his fault, but August reassures him that it was May who caused her own death and no one else.

Zach and August begin to drape the hives as a sign of mourning May's death. August explains that this is a beekeeping tradition. August tells Lily the story of Aristaeus, which is considered to be the second part of the beekeeping initiation. Aristaeus was the first beekeeper, and all of his bees died, but they were reborn out of a sacrificed bull. After this miracle, people believed that bees had power over death. The presence of bees symbolizes the rebirth of a dead person in the next world. August confesses that draping the hives is not for May but for the mourners. She says that the drapes remind them that life gives way to death and death gives way to life.

The Daughters of Mary visit with an abundance of food. They comment about how good May looks, and they make jokes about the white "drive through" funeral homes that have started springing up. Lily was thrilled that they made the joke freely and did not consider apologizing because of her presence. Lily truly feels that she has become one of them. Lily decides that if she should die, she would want to be put in a display window so that the Daughters could drive by and laugh.

August finds May's suicide note. May apologizes for leaving them in such a manner, and she says that she is just too tired of carrying around the weight of the world. She adds that it is her time to die, but it is June's and August's time to live. She encourages them not to mess up their chance. August interprets the note as an encouragement to June to marry Neil. June seems to take this advice to heart, and she thinks deeply.

Zach, Lily, and August undrape the hives, and they begin to feel more comfortable with the idea of saying goodbye to May. Neil is often at the Boatwright house, but he seems confused by the way June stares at him. The rest of the house also watches the interaction between Neil and June. May's funeral is surrounded by the hum of bees, a sound Lily determines to be the sound of souls flying away.

Analysis

August's explanation that "hot weather makes the bees out of sorts" foreshadows the crazy water fight that ensues shortly afterward. Since bees parallel the human world in this novel, it is to be expected that people will act out of sorts in the heat as well. The women uncharacteristically have a water fight, acting like children, running, and yelling. For most of them, this type of activity might have seemed within the realm of possibility, and it is good to see May in a burst of frivolity. June's character prior to this point would never have allowed for this type of silly behavior. Yet, this scene brings her to understand something about Lily, and June seems to finally accept Lily in the household.

The other conflicts in Lily's life continue on their path toward resolution. She solidifies her understanding of her mother's presence at the Boatwrights', even though the revelation of facts she might have guessed drives her close to insanity. Despite her constant attempts to not think about her mother, all Lily can think about is where her mother sat, stood, and worked around the pink house. At this point, Lily is pulled apart by a new conflict. On the one hand, Lily is quite happy and content in her new life at the Boatwright house, and her relationship with Zach is good overall. On the other hand, Lily feels anguished by the uncertainty of what happened with her mother and realizes that living there will constantly bring reminders of her mother.

After Zach is jailed, we see August as a woman who is not just pleasant and hospitable but also ready to fight when necessary, having a fire in her belly. Prior to this incident, she seemingly was content with the world, laid back, and willing to let the world take her where it needed. Now, August is angered by the injustice of what happened to Zach, and she displays the will to fight. Rosaleen has a fire in her too, but a different kind. Kidd uses simile to compare August's fire to a hearth and Rosaleen's fire to the type that burns down a house.

Lily recalls that she saw May building "an addition" to her wall. This statement foreshadows May's eventual death. The wall symbolizes May's pain, and therefore an addition to it would symbolize more pain. May begins to carry an unbearable weight of the pain of the world, which ultimately leads to her suicide. Even before receiving the news about Zach, May probably felt the sorrow shared by the others, and she likely considered suicide even before talking with Zach's mother on the phone. The last straw for May, though, was realizing that she was not accepted as an equal in the household; everyone was hiding the news from her, marginalizing her and acknowledging that something serious was wrong with her. This act of protection, however, was probably more of an insult to May's autonomy. Indeed, the others saw the suicide coming, more or less.

At May's wake, Sugar-Girl makes a joke about "white people's funeral homes" without any consideration for the fact that Lily is white. It is at this turning point that Lily feels she has become one of the Daughters regardless of race, just as the one man in group was not excluded because of his gender. Lily begins to wish that skin color was not a factor at all in human existence—after all, the bees in a hive do not have to worry about looking different from one another—and she begins to take a clearer view of the evil nature of the ways people often handle racial differences.

Summary and Analysis of Chapters 11 and 12

August stops all beekeeping as she and June continue to mourn. Rosaleen cooks all of the meals. Lily is now ready to talk to August, but she forbears because of August's grief. Lily occupies her time by writing in her notebook, and before long she fills up all of the pages. She walks in the woods and wonders about her mother. She considers where she and Rosaleen might go next. Often, Lily does not want to get out of bed at all.

June has begun taking long car rides with Neil. Zach visits on occasion, and seeing him causes Lily's stomach to turn circles. Lily tells him that she considers him a friend, a boyfriend, a beekeeper, and a brother. She tells him what would happen if she were black, but Zach replies that there is no use in that kind of speculation. Instead they have to think about changing the world. Lily discovers something in him that has grown angry, and he fills his mind with complex race-relation issues. Lily wishes they could return back to the simple conversations they had before.

At dinner one night, Rosaleen directly asks June whether or not she will marry Neil. June will not answer. After dinner they say Hail Marys for the first time since May's death.

Lily decides to move back into the honey house because she has missed having a room to herself. Lily is determined that the next day she will tell August the truth about her background. She is consumed by fear all night.

She sleeps late and awakens to the smell of cake. She walks into the kitchen to see Rosaleen, June, and August baking and singing. They explain that they are baking to celebrate Mary Day, the day that Mary rose up to heaven. The day serves as a remembrance day for Our Lady, and May named it Mary Day. Much work is required for the preparation of Mary Day: decoration, food, and of course the chaining of Mary. They have begun to decorate when Neil shows up at the door, asking for a word with June. Once again, Neil asks June to marry him, and this time June says yes. June and Neil leave immediately to go pick out a ring. August, Rosaleen, and Lily bubble over with excitement. As they prepare for the celebration, Lily is fascinated by seeing Zach mowing the lawn shirtless, even though she tries not to look.

June returns in the evening with her engagement ring, and everyone compliments its beauty. The Daughters come over to the house, and they feast. Lily determines to talk to August that night, and she realizes her intense love for her life in Tiburon. Lunelle offers to make her a hat like the hats of the other Daughters, and Lily is honored. They all eat Mary's honey cakes, feeding each other the cakes. June apologizes to Lily for having given her a hard time at the beginning of her stay. August retells the story of black Mary while Otis and Neil chain Mary to the honey house.

Zach catches Lily's eye and eventually holds her hand. Lily tells Zach that she used to be harassed by boys who would put live fish around her neck, forcing Lily either to swim to let the fish live, or to get out of the water and kill the fish. The fish would ultimately die against her. Lily also confronts Zach about how he has changed since being in jail. Zach confesses he gets angry, but he promises Lily that he will not become mean. Zach kisses Lily, and she loves everything about the kiss. Zach resolves to study hard this year and be able to go to college, and Lily assures him that he will succeed. Zach promises Lily that though they cannot be together now, after he becomes something he will come back for her. He gives her a dog tag with his name on it so that she will not forget.

The Daughters of Mary tease Zach and Lily for going off on their own. Lily waits for August in her room in order to finally come clean. Lily takes notice of the artwork, the books, and the items in August's room. Lily is most taken aback by a book of pictures of Mary being given a lily by the angel Gabriel.

August enters her bedroom, and Lily takes out the photo of her mother. August insists that she looks just like her mother. August knew exactly who her mother was. August confesses that as soon as Lily told August her name, August knew exactly who she was. Lily asks why August did not bring it up sooner, but August insists that everything comes with time.

August tells Lily that she was a housekeeper in Deborah's house. Deborah loved peanut butter and dolls but hated schoolwork. Lily also confesses that she lied about her father being dead. August knows his name, and Lily explains that he is a bad father. She tells August that T. Ray insisted that her mother left both T. Ray and Lily. Lily cries against August and says that she did not believe T. Ray; she set out to prove him wrong. Lily also divulges the details about Rosaleen's arrest. Lily says that she is a bad person, having done so many wrong things, yet all of this is nothing compared to her worst sin: she killed her mother. Lily feels unlovable. August reassures her, however, that not only Zach but also all the Boatwrights and Daughters of Mary, even June, all love Lily.

Lily explains how she was able to find the Boatwrights using the black Mary picture and matching the picture with the honey label. August exclaims that it is almost as if Lily was meant to find them. Lily says that she is sure about that.

August describes her interaction with Lily's mother. She explains how she began working for Deborah's mother, Sarah, when Deborah was four years old. She worked there for nine years and then began teaching. When she left for South Carolina, Deborah was nineteen years old and was devastated that she left. Deborah moved to Sylvan, following the advice of a high school friend. Deborah met T. Ray there, and they were married. Lily questions why she would marry him, and August insists that he started off a good man; Deborah loved him. However, August points out, people change after life gets through with them. Besides, when T. Ray first proposed, Deborah had rejected the proposal, but she later changed her mind because she was pregnant.

Lily panics and realizes she was an unwanted baby. Lily wishes she never knew that. August reassures Lily that her mother said that Lily was such a pretty baby that it made her eyes hurt. August discusses what Lily always hoped to hear: that her mother had loved her and cared for her. August says that she thinks her mother was happy for a while, before her life changed toward unhappiness. She wrote to August saying she was leaving T. Ray, and she asked if she could stay with the Boatwrights for a while. She came to the house without Lily because she was depressed and falling apart.

Lily now decides that she hates her mother for leaving her behind. August attempts to reason with her, but Lily insists that she does hate her. Lily thinks it was easy for her mother to leave her since she was an unwanted baby in the first place. August explains that Deborah arrived to Tiburon as skin and bone. She would not eat and was depressed. August attempts to explain that people who are depressed do things they normally would not do. Lily flips back and forth between hating her mother and pitying her. Once Deborah's condition improved, August continues, Deborah decided she would go back to Sylvan to get Lily.

Suddenly, Lily's memory of the day her mother died seems new. In fact, Deborah had returned to get Lily, not just to get her belongings. Lily is angered by the fact that they did not get away from T. Ray that day. August continues, saying that she called the house to find out what happened to Deborah. A neighbor informed her of Deborah's death. August tried to learn more, but T. Ray would not offer any information.

Lily feels that her new knowledge is a curse. She has the truth, but it is heavy. August reassures Lily that everyone makes mistakes, and her mother did the best she could to rectify the situation. August explains that nothing is perfect, and "there is only life."

Analysis

Mary Day allows for a break in the grief following May's death. The celebration adds significant symbolism to Lily's life. Mary's binding in chains parallels Lily's consistent restraint due to her uncertainty about her mother. Lily is bound to wonder and be confused, to fail to know the truth. Mary will become unbound, and so too will Lily. That Mary escapes her chains foreshadows the fact that Lily will soon learn the truth behind her mother's life and death.

Lily's story about the boys harassing her and giving her a necklace of a live fish parallels her relationship with Zach. In the fish story, Lily has to decide whether to stay in the water and save the fish or to get out of the water and kill the fish. In her relationship with Zach, Lily knows that staying with him will be painful for both of them, for the world will not accept them as a couple. Yet, not being with him would also be painful, since both of them care for each other so deeply.

Throughout Lily's discussion with August about Deborah, Deborah's character is developed posthumously. Prior to this point, the reader's understanding of Deborah has been limited to her relationship with Lily. Finally, during this conversation, August explains Deborah's personality as a child and a young woman. August fills in the missing pieces that Lily needs. It is not quite a flashback, because this is a conversation about the past, not a narrative shift to a different time, but the majority of the conversation seems to focus on the events of the past.

This conversation demonstrates to Lily the burden of knowledge. Here readers might recall the story of Oedipus, who killed his own father and spends the majority of [Oedipus Rex] in a struggle for knowledge about the truth of his past, only to discover the horrible truth and then have to live with it. Though Lily now knows what happened to her mother, she is saddened by the truth that she at first was unwanted and that her mother subsequently left her to go to Tiburon. (Despite the serious mood of this moment, Kidd manages to add humor to the scene when Lily confesses her aspiration to be an amnesiac, preferring to forget the truth.)

August has been burdened with this knowledge from the beginning, but the burden has been comparatively light because August was not herself the subject of Deborah's actions. Instead, August has been the prudent and patient one, first taking in Deborah and then taking in Deborah's daughter ten years later. Still, we must wonder how the new revelations from Lily feel for August, who is learning for the first time that Lily killed her own mother and that Rosaleen has been a fugitive from the law. These revelations probably seem less important to August than the news that June is finally going to get married and less important to August than the death of their other sister, May.

As for Lily, she is pulled in two directions by her mother's story. On the one hand, Lily is furious with her mother for leaving Sylvan to come to Tiburon without her. On the other hand, Lily knows that she returned in order to get Lily before she died, which makes her deserving of love, respect, and pity. Against these feelings, Lily finally is confronting the fact that she picked up the gun and killed her mother. Although it was an accident, she is furious with herself.

Summary and Analysis of Chapters 13 and 14

Lily remains in August's room alone. Lily tries to force herself to sleep, but she cannot. Lily goes to see Our Lady, bound up in chains, and fights the desire to release her from the chains. She imagines that her mother's endless love is outside of the honey house. Lily feels angry but also feels that she has no right to be angry. She begins to pace, and in her anger she throws a honey jar against the table—then another and another until there are no more jars and the room is a mess. She moves on to candles and a bucket.

Lily feels tremendous sadness, not so much over her destruction of the honey house but over being behind by her mother. She lies down on her cot and drifts to sleep, waking the next morning to Rosaleen shaking her. Lily explains that she threw the honey, much to Rosaleen's disappointment. Rosaleen nurses Lily's self-inflicted wound. Rosaleen tells Lily that she had feared Lily would discover the sad truth, having heard rumors that Deborah had left. Lily is upset that Rosaleen did not explain this to her earlier, but Rosaleen assures her that she did not want to hurt Lily. Rosaleen and Lily clean up the honey house without speaking a word to each other.

The Daughters (including Otis) show up for the second day of the celebration, but Lily isolates herself from the group—even from Zach. Lily notices that August is watching her actions, and she thinks that somehow August knows about the honey house disaster. Lily asks August to tell Zach the true story of Lily's past, for Lily cannot. While listening to the music of the Our Lady celebration, Lily envisions her mother getting on the bus to leave her in Sylvan.

As the ceremony continues, Neil and Zach carry the Our Lady statue out of the honey house, and August reads Mary's words from the Bible. August explains that the celebration commemorates Mary rising to heaven. She also emphasizes that Mary was always able to break the chains that have bound her. As a group, the Daughters and others begin removing the chains from Mary. August announces that Mary cannot be cast down, and neither can her daughters.

August then opens a jar of Black Madonna Honey and pours it over the head of the Our Lady statue. The Daughters begin rubbing the honey into the statue, and soon Lily joins in as well. The Daughters explain that churches bathe their statues in holy water, but the Daughters use honey. Honey, as a preservative, symbolizes how Mary's spirit will be preserved in the hearts of the Daughters. All of the women fall into a rhythm of massaging honey into Our Lady. Lily realizes that this is the first time since she learned the truth about her mother that she has felt content doing anything. After the washing, Lily lays down on a cot attempting not to think.

August enters the honey house with a box full of Deborah's things. The two of them open the box together and examine the contents. Inside August finds a pocket mirror, which August says would reflect her mother's face. There is also a hairbrush with a hair attached to it. Despite Lily's anger at her mother, she is still overcome with emotion at the seeing a part of her mother's actual body. August hands Lily a whale pin that Deborah wore on her first day in Tiburon. Next, August hands Lily a book of English poetry that she had loaned to Deborah during her stay in Tiburon. The last item in the box is a photo of Deborah leaning toward a baby Lily in a high chair. Lily is obsessed with every detail of the photo, but mostly she considers the photo to be the sign that she was looking for, a sign of love from Deborah herself.

Lily stays to herself after receiving her mother's belongings. When she puts the hatbox under her bed, Lily finds a pile of mouse bones. She carries the bones around with her for a reason she does not know. Lily obsesses over where her mother may have stepped, may have sat, may have ate… She grieves intensely, and the Boatwrights give her time to soak in her pain.

June sets an October 10 wedding date. Rosaleen offers to bake the cake. One afternoon, Lily sees June and August clinging to each other, crying about how May would have loved the upcoming wedding. The next day, Rosaleen tells Lily that she is going to register to vote. Lily worries that Rosaleen's name might be recognized as a criminal's name, but Rosaleen insists. Lily declines to come along but regrets her choice. She particularly regrets not taking the opportunity to tell Rosaleen she is proud of her.

Lily decides to call Zach, and he apologizes for all that she has been through. He reassures her that if she had to go back to T. Ray, he would visit her. He tells her that he will be attending a white high school this coming school year, and Lily determines that both of them are doomed.

Rosaleen calls all of the Daughters to tell them that she has registered to vote. Lily still regrets not going along. Lily ties up her mouse bones and sets them aside, figuring that she may have just needed to nurse something.

The next morning, Lily wears her mother's whale pin and goes out to the hives with August. August shows Lily a hive with no queen. The bees are lethargic and uninterested in their usual business. August suggests that perhaps Our Lady could be a stand-in mother for Lily in the place of Deborah. August explains that the power of Mary is not constrained within a statue, but rather the power is inside of her. Mary encourages people to pursue the most important purpose in life: to persist in love.

Lily begins to write in a new notebook from Zach. She outlines the details of everything that has taken place since Mary Day. Upon hearing a knock, Lily opens the front door of the Boatwright house to find T. Ray staring at her. T. Ray threatens to take Lily back home no matter what. Lily asks T. Ray how he found her. T. Ray explains that he was able to track her using the phone bill, and Miss Lacey was happy to provide the rest.

T. Ray notices the pin Lily is wearing and asks where Lily got it. T. Ray says that he gave the pin to Deborah, so Lily explains that Deborah had been at the Boatwrights' house when she left Sylvan. T. Ray becomes frustrated, saying he looked all over for her. Lily realizes how much he must have loved Deborah and imagines that he turned ugly only after she left.

T. Ray slaps Lily across the face and begins yelling at her as if she is Deborah. He screams about her leaving and even refers to Lily as "Deborah." Lily finally calls him "Daddy" in order to snap him out of his hallucination. Lily sees August and Rosaleen, but she decides to deal with this on her own. Lily calmly reassures T. Ray that she is fine. T. Ray tells her that they are going home, but Lily insists that she will not be going home with him.

August steps in to mediate. She tells T. Ray that Lily is welcome to stay with the Boatwrights as long as she wants. Lily can tell that T. Ray does not want Lily around to remind him of Deborah anyway. Eventually T. Ray leaves, allowing Lily to stay. As his truck backs out of the driveway, Lily runs after him, demanding to know if she really killed her mother. T. Ray assures her that although she did do it, it was an accident.

Lily wonders if she will hear from T. Ray again. In the fall, she receives her hat from Lunelle, and Clayton works out Rosaleen and her criminal case. At school, Clayton's daughter Becca and Lily are both friends with Zach despite the bad reputation they get. Lily forgives both herself and her mother. She is responsible for maintaining May's wall, and she finds Mary's spirit at unexpected moments. Overall, Lily feels most lucky to have so many mothers who love her.

Analysis

Lily's destruction of the honey house is a final outburst of the emotions she has been carrying with her throughout the novel. She felt rage, sadness, confusion, and loss all along, but once she learned the whole truth from August, all of these feelings come to a boil. Throughout the novel, it is clear that besides writing, Lily has very little outlet for her emotions. Therefore, it is fitting that she lets them all out in a completely destructive and arbitrary manner. Ironically, in the process of destroying the honey house, she is crushing what she loves in order to express her feelings.

The building itself remains, however, and this (in addition to the people who knew Deborah) is the key continuity between Lily and her mother. Later, Lily receives additional tokens of her mother's presence at the house. When August presents Lily with her mother's hairbrush with a hair attached, Lily's hardened exterior falls apart, and her soft, tender, vulnerable side is exposed. Despite Lily's varying feelings about her mother, witnessing an actual part of her body brings new, even stronger feelings into Lily's heart. Then, when Lily receives the photo of Lily and her mother, her feelings toward her mother completely change. The anger begins to subside, and she begins to feel grief and true loss, for she has seen the sign of motherly love she has been looking for.

Lily even carries the mouse bones, which could be old enough to be from a mouse her mother once saw. It is true that, as Lily says, sometimes people just need something to take care of. At different points in the novel, Lily has been taken care of by various people. Yet, she was rarely given the opportunity to look after others. Nevertheless, the mouse bones might have a distant connection to her mother. Sometimes people do unexpected things because of their emotions. Lily is feeling sentimental enough to do something that might seem crazy, and she seems unclear about why the bones might signify something special about her mother. Remember that unlike May, Deborah has not been properly viewed or mourned by Lily, and perhaps the bones also reflect a kind of presence, like the hair from the brush, that proves that Deborah has moved on.

In any case, Lily finds better solace in rubbing honey into Our Lady. The act of rubbing the honey into the statue symbolizes preservation. Lily had longed to preserve her mother for her entire life, and by preserving Mary, a stand-in mother, Lily is able to feel power over her emotions once again. Additionally, she is not facing this task alone. Rather, she is in sync with the Daughters, her new extended family.

At the end of the novel, Lily truly has an understanding for motherhood. Though she still feels grief over killing her mother, she is reassured that Deborah loved her. Additionally, she has found eight new mothers to care for her and love her with overwhelming passion, kindness, and deep love.

The novel thus ends on a note of promise. Zach is taking steps to integrate with white society, and he is helped along by Lily, who appreciates him for what he is. Lily also has come to terms with who she is; she is not so much her father's daughter anymore but belongs to her new mothers. She has gone through a catharsis of grief and is ready to move forward.

Suggested Essay Questions

1. **What are some of the ways that bees serve as symbols in Lily's life?**

   Answer:

   a) Bees symbolize Lily's mother in a number of instances throughout the novel. In Sylvan, Lily feels her mother's presence when swarms of bees enter her room. Her mother's name, Deborah, literally translates as "bee." She follows the path of her mother to Tiburon and finds herself on a honey farm.

   b) Bees model human society. Once Lily begins her beekeeper training with August, she quickly learns the ways in which a beehive models the human world. Lily learns to send the bees love, to act like she knows what she's doing, and to avoid angry outbursts--all reasonably good lessons for life.

   c) Bees, like Lily, need a queen or a mother figure in order to function. At the beginning of the novel, Lily uses the memory of her mother as this figure. Lily sometimes depends on Rosaleen to fulfill this role, and once in Tiburon, Lily mainly counts on August. Eventually, she turns to all eight of her Tiburon "mothers" to fulfill this need in her life.

2. **Why does Lily feel the need to carry around mouse bones with her?**

   Answer: Lily finds the mouse bones under her bed when she is storing her mother's belongings. Therefore, Lily makes some odd connection between the mouse bones and the sentimental day on which she learned of her mother's love for her. Lily is in an emotionally heightened state, and she therefore displays some seemingly irrational behavior. After Lily finishes babysitting the mouse bones, she determines that she may have just needed to nurse something. But she might have intuited that the bones could be from a mouse Deborah once saw. In addition, the bones could symbolize Deborah's dead body.

3. **How does Lily's idea of a mother change throughout the novel?**

   Answer: In the beginning of the novel, Lily associates the idea of "mother" only with a legal and biological connection between a woman and her child. She displays this definition when she dreams of Rosaleen adopting her and becoming her "real mother." But Lily's relationship with her biological mother is based on memories and uncertainty. Lily spends the majority of her childhood attempting to put together the missing pieces in her mother's life. Such curiosity drives Lily to travel to Tiburon. Lily experiences feelings of anger, pity, and grief when she learns the true story of her own mother.

Along the way, Lily also recognizes Our Lady in Chains as the mother of all, including her. She looks to Mary as a mother who brings about the inner strength inside Lily.

Finally, Lily is able to connect the term "mother" to the eight women in Tiburon who have pledged their love, time, and resources to ensure that she has the best life possible. Now, a mother in her mind is someone who takes up the role of a mother.

4. **What does the symbol of Our Lady of Chains provide for the Daughters of Mary?**

Answer: The Daughters of Mary, as a group of black women in the South in the 1960s, have clearly been exposed to their share of discrimination. The Boatwright sisters have attended college, but they have not really been able to find appropriate jobs outside of the black community, except for domestic positions within white households. The women feel the societal chains that bind them to a specific status position. The story of Our Lady provides women with hope for advancing their lives regardless of the "chains" that hold them down. Rather, they realize their ability to harness their internal power to enhance their lives.

5. **What are some examples of characters suffering from the "burden of knowing"?**

Answer: Lily feels terrible pain when she learns the truth about her mother temporarily leaving her behind. Lily feels that she would rather go back to the point in her life when she could just wonder about the truth, given that the truth hurts her so much. She is forced to move forward with this new information anyway. When she sees the photograph depicting her as a baby interacting with Deborah, however, she then realizes her mother loved her. Suddenly, she is hurt again, but in a new way because she feels a great loss due to her mother's death, and she realizes even more strongly how her own killing of her mother has caused this loss.

May feels a great burden from perceiving the pain of the world. She is weighed down when others are hurt. She does her best to alleviate the pain through rituals like putting notes in the wailing wall. Her family attempts to shield her from knowledge that will hurt her further. But when she does learn the truth about Zach, the burden becomes too heavy, for she also learns what everyone else thinks about her frailty, and she ultimately kills herself.

August, for her part, feels the burden of knowing that Lily's story is false, yet August is willing to shoulder this burden in patience until Lily is ready to talk.

6. **How does Lily's concept of race evolve throughout the novel?**

Answer: Lily begins the novel having a close relationship with Rosaleen, her black housekeeper. Still, she does not consider white people and black people to be equal. When she arrives in Tiburon, however, she realizes her own prejudices. She discovers that she has believed that she did not believe that a black person could be as smart as she is. Her idea was disproved once she met August. She also is angry when June discriminates against her for being white. She begins to understand discrimination and begins to be able to empathize. Then, when Lily falls for Zach, she is overcome with curiosity and confusion that she could be attracted to a black man. Yet, she soon realizes her deep and lasting feelings for him and sees him for who he is. Despite their love, Lily learns that they cannot truly be together because of the racial divide between them, and she comes to understand the equality of people as well as the curse of racism. When she is fully accepted by the Daughters of Mary and fully appreciates the Black Madonna, we can say that she has become fully integrated into a world (as yet unrealized elsewhere) where race does not matter for getting along with others in equality and love.

7. **What causes T. Ray to become so bitter and abusive toward Lily?**

Answer: Lily's mother and T. Ray had seemingly been truly in love when they first began their relationship. August tells Lily that Deborah said that T. Ray treated her like a princess, and they conceived a child. Deborah finally agreed to marry T. Ray after she was pregnant. Yet, at some point in their marriage, their relationship turned sour. Deborah fell into depression, the cause of which is uncertain. Deborah eventually left her Sylvan home with Lily to escape to Tiburon. Lily determines that when Deborah left, it must have effectively killed T. Ray, which would explain his harsh attitude and bitterness. Additionally, Deborah's death must have caused T. Ray great sadness. Now that Lily has grown to be a teenager, she looks more and more like Deborah. T. Ray takes out his anger towards Deborah on Lily, most clearly demonstrated at the end of the novel, when he actually addresses Lily as Deborah.

8. **Discuss why and how Lily is torn about her sense of home after she arrives in Tiburon.**

Answer: Lily loves her new life in Tiburon. She loves her work in the honey house, her relationship with the Boatwright sisters, and her interactions with Zach. She finds herself happy keeping her life a secret and keeping the facade she has created. Yet, despite her utopian life in Tiburon, Lily cannot help but wonder what T. Ray is going through back in Sylvan. After all, despite T. Ray's horrible treatment of Lily, he is the only real parent whom Lily has known. Lily wonders if he misses her, if he worries about her, and if he feels guilty for her treatment of her. Due to this curiosity, Lily surrenders to her urges and calls T. Ray, which ultimately leads him to find her in Tiburon.

9. **How does Lily's relationship with Zach expand her understanding of herself and of society?**

Answer: Once Lily begins her relationship with Zach, she learns that she has the capability to love a boy. Additionally, she is fascinated by the thought that she is capable of becoming so enamored by a black boy, a situation she had never thought possible. She begins to become more in touch with her own body as it is evolving into womanhood. She also more clearly understands her feelings, her urges, and her fears. Zach provides her with a solid sense of self, of confidence, and of hope for her future. Lily also learns that society will not always make room for love. Societal views in the time and place of the novel would never permit a relationship between a young interracial couple. Lily learns that despite her mutual feelings with Zach, the nation needs some sort of revolution before it will accept their relationship.

10. **August tells Lily that the most important purpose of life is to "persist in love." How does August exemplify her own words?**

Answer: August has lived an unmarried life, but she is in no way alone. From her childhood, she has always been surrounded by the love of her family. August returns that love unconditionally. She discusses her intense love and her sorrow concerning April. She consistently tolerates the narrow-minded opinions of June, and she does everything she can to provide May with as much relief from pain as possible. She is clearly the leader of the family, for she runs the honey farm, bringing in the majority of the income. At the same time, however, August represents the emotional leadership in the family, holding the other women as they cry, laughing with them, and providing unconditional love. At a time when it would be easier not to do so, August provided great love for Deborah, even after she finished working with the Fontanel family. A generation later, August allows Lily to stay with her, persisting in love for Deborah. She loves Lily despite her lies, her anger, and her sadness. She ultimately makes a great sacrifice, taking Lily and Rosaleen into her household, because she loves them. (Remember the positive meanings of the word "august," which also relate to August.)

Honey as a Healer

Upon arriving at the Boatwright house, Lily learns the benefit of adding honey to her diet and her beauty regimen. Her skinny limbs begin to plump, and her hair begins to soften. The doses of honey seem to do wonders for her body. Through both topical application and through ingestion, honey might have numerous health benefits for a variety of ailments from burns to digestion. Honey apparently has been shown to increase longevity, and beekeepers perhaps have statistically fewer incidents of cancer and arthritis than any other occupational group.

The use of honey for healing has been a practice for over 5,000 years. Ancient Greeks used to dab the sticky substance onto wounds in order to heal them more quickly. For the most common of ailments, honey can be used to speed up the healing process. For instance, for natural sunburn relief, combine 1 cup of apple cider vinegar, 1/4 cup of honey, and 1/4 cup of Aloe Vera gel, and apply the mixture to the sunburned skin. Honey also has a high potassium content, which helps honey kill bacteria. Therefore, applying a thin layer of honey to cuts and scrapes can help keep out bacteria, in addition to providing something of a barrier against the air.

Today, honey is not just a common home remedy; honey products are being marketed to physicians for use in the treatment of burns and wounds. MEDIHONEY dressings, for instance, use Leptospermum honey to help remove dead skin tissue and thus facilitate the growth of new cells. The dressings are the first FDA-approved honey-based product for wounds, and they have been used for a while in the UK, Australia, and New Zealand. They are just recently being introduced to the United States market.

Honey has also been shown to combat infections due to its bacteria-killing property. Honey sometimes can destroy infections that are typically immune to drug treatment, such as group A streptococcus, a flesh eating bacteria, and methicillin-resistant *Staphylococcus aureus*, which causes thousands of deaths every year. Using honey for these bacteria has not yet become common practice, but physicians who have tried everything else are sometimes able to find hope in honey.

Of course, honey also can be ingested for its nutritional value. Eating honey is said to do wonders to assist with a person's sleeping habits. A spoonful before bed is said to assist children in avoiding bed wetting, and mixing it with milk before bed can help adults with insomnia. A teaspoon of honey per day apparently can increase calcium intake and therefore decrease the risk of diseases such as osteoporosis. In addition, the use of honey is common in dispelling sore throats or coughs, often being mixed with lemon or tea. Other use honey to combat nasal congestion by combining it with boiling water and then breathing in the fumes.

Finally, honey has been used to increase the health of skin and hair. For a deep facial cleanser, some people mix honey with oatmeal as a face mask. Others make honey into a hair conditioner by mixig it with olive oil.

Whether these remedies and processes work as advertised or not, honey certainly can be added to the healthy person's repertoire.

Author of ClassicNote and Sources

Adena Raub, author of ClassicNote. Completed on September 04, 2008, copyright held by GradeSaver.

Updated and revised Adam Kissel November 30, 2008. Copyright held by GradeSaver.

Sue Monk Kidd. The Secret Life of Bees. New York: Penguin Books, 2002.

"An Interview with Sue Monk Kidd." 2008-03-14.
<http://www.bookbrowse.com/author_interviews/full/index.cfm?author_number=820>.

"Sue Monk Kidd." 2008-03-19. <http://www.suemonkkidd.com>.

South Carolina Mid-Atlantic Beekeepers Association, "Beekeeping Glossary." South Carolina Mid-Atlantic Beekeepers Association. 2006-12-12. 2008-08-24.
<http://www.midstatebeekeepers.com/education.html#glossary>.

Penguin Group. "The Secret Life of Bees." 2008-01-01. 2008-09-04.
<http://us.penguingroup.com/nf/Book/BookDisplay/0,,9780670032372,00.html>.

Katherine H. Wyrick. "The buzz on Sue Monk Kidd's dazzling fictional debut." BookPage. 2002-01-01. 2008-09-04.
<http://www.bookpage.com/0202bp/sue_monk_kidd.html>.

Colin Boyd. "Movie Trailer - Queen Latifah and Dakota Fanning in 'The Secret Life of Bees'." GetTheBigPicture.Net. 2008-01-01. 2008-09-04.
<http://www.getthebigpicture.net/blog/2008/8/20/movie-trailer-queen-latifah-and-dakota-fanning-in-the-secret.html>.

Christine Baker. "The Secret Life of Bees." Brigham Young University. 2008-01-01. 2008-09-04.
<http://english.byu.edu/Novelinks/Novel%20Pages/Secret%20Life%20of%20Bees.htm>.

La Vie en Rose. "Sue Monk Kidd Interview." La Vie en Rose. 2005-01-01. 2008-09-04.
<http://www.lverose.com/mind-body-spirit/bookclub/monkkidd-interview.htm>.

Kelly Joyce Neff. "The healing power of honey: From burns to weak bones, raw honey can help ." NaturalNews. 2007-01-26. 2008-09-04.
<http://www.naturalnews.com/021506.html>.

Elizabeth Cole. "The Healing Power of Honey." The Frugal Life. 2008-01-01. 2008-09-04. <http://www.thefrugallife.com/honey.html>.

DermaSciences, Inc. "Ancient Healing Power: Honey Makes Sweet Comeback in Treating Advanced Wounds." MedicalNewsToday. 2007-10-24. 2008-09-04. <http://www.medicalnewstoday.com/articles/86527.php>.

Brandon Keim. "Honey Remedy Could Save Limbs." Wired.Com. 2006-10-11. 2008-09-04. <http://www.wired.com/medtech/health/news/2006/10/71925>.

Essay: The Concept of Monomyth in Kidd's Secret Life of Bees

by Anonymous
May 06, 2007

In Sue Monk Kidd's The Secret Life of Bees, Joseph Campbell's concept of the monomyth is employed to develop Lily's journey from a lack of familial recognition and worthlessness into a new life of true meaning and appreciation. Joseph Campbell argues that all stories are essentially the same because of their relation to the monomyth. Throughout this journey, the hero undergoes three critical phases, which include the departure, initiation, and return. They must overcome barriers and may drift away into peril, but will eventually gain the freedom to live. Along with applying the theory of monomyth to works of fiction, Campbell also utilized the idea of archetypes created by Carl Jung. He used them to discover the profound meanings behind myth and religion. More importantly, these archetypes are present in novels to express the collective unconscious and are a significant part of the hero's journey.

In every monomyth, the hero must first leave his or her home in order to embark on an empowering journey. This first step is known as the departure. In Kidd's novel, Lily follows many of the same steps of the departure as were described by Joseph Campbell. Lily's first action in the voyage is when she is called to the adventure. After T. Ray takes Lily home from jail, she is sent to her room; they engage in an argument concerning Lily's mother. T. Ray laughs, " 'The woman could have cared less about you.' Lily says, 'That's not true, it's not'" (Kidd 39). After this indignant comment from T. Ray, Lily feels completely empty inside. Throughout her entire young life, Lily has lacked a strong mother archetype and is now realizing that she must go on a sort of journey in order to re-establish this archetype within her collective unconscious. Many heroes are also given the help of something that is beyond their world, a type of paranormal support. Joseph Campbell states that another move along the road of departure includes the assistance of a supernatural aid. As Lily is sitting in her room after T. Ray scolds her, she hears a voice inside her head. Lily thinks, " I heard a voice say, Lily Melissa Owens, your jar is open. In a matter of seconds I knew exactly what I had to do- leave" (Kidd 41). Lily is given the incentive to leave the house from the voice inside her head. To her, it transforms into a rare opportunity in which she is given justification to abandon her home and do better for herself. Later in the novel, August describes the sound that Lily hears in her mind as the voice of Mary.

Throughout the duration of the novel, Lily applies this voice within herself as a guide that leads her down the path of her unconscious mind. Now that Lily has decided that she must leave T. Ray, she must take her first steps away from home. Campbell refers to this stage of the departure as crossing the first threshold. Lily crosses this limit after she gathers all of her possessions and writes a letter to T. Ray. Lily's letter says, "'Dear T. Ray, don't bother looking for me. Lily. P.S. People who tell lies like you should rot in hell'"(Kidd 42). Lily has truly crossed the point of no return; she now must disappear because after T. Ray finds this letter, she knows he will severely punish her. She has no alternative other than to continue on her journey away from home.

Campbell refers to the first challenge of the hero as "the belly of the whale." This experience will test the will of the hero and supply him or her with the necessary ideals to continue. Lily encounters her first major test after she decides that she must free Rosaleen. Lily goes to the hospital to which Rosaleen has been consigned and proceeds to call a nurse in the colored section of the hospital while pretending to be the jailer's wife. Lily states, " 'Mr. Gaston wants you to send the policeman that we've got there back to the station. Tell him the preacher is on his way to sign some papers, and Mr. Gaston can't be here cause he had to leave just now'" (Kidd 48). With the policeman gone, Lily and Rosaleen are able to escape. Telling such a lie was a difficult test for Lily because she must defy the law in order to help Rosaleen escape. This trial shows that Lily is competent and has the will power she needs in order to complete her adventure. At this point in the novel, Lily has completed the stage of departure. The situations that Lily must overcome in the steps of the departure show how Lily is following Campbell's theory of monomyth.

There is a significant amount of evidence that the initiation phase of the monomyth exists in The Secret Life of Bees. Lily begins the road of trials when she starts the journey to August's house. During this journey, Lily begins her terrible habit of lying. Lily tells a lie to a salesman that she meets, right before finding out where her mother received the picture of the black Mary. " 'I don't believe I've seen you before,' he said. 'I'm not from around here. I'm visiting my grandmother'" (Kidd 62). Lily has begun to step out of her normal routine by telling lies, which is something that she would have never done back at her home with T. Ray because she knew it was morally wrong and unethical. Shortly after reaching August's house, Lily has the meeting with the goddess, or god in this case. This character serves as another role in Campbell's monomyth. Lily is instantly charmed by Zachary's looks and behavior. Lily thought, "At my school they made fun of colored people's lips and noses. I myself had laughed at these jokes, hoping to fit in. Now I wished I could pen a letter to my school to be read at opening assembly that would tell them how wrong we'd all been" (Kidd 116). Zachary is Lily's god in the story, because she consistently finds him amazing and lovable. To Lily, Zach is flawless; he is a substitute father figure in a way, because he possesses all of the positive, upstanding qualities that T. Ray lacks as a father. Once Lily realizes that Zach has all of these qualities she has never admired in a male before, Zach becomes her god. Not only does Lily have Zach to distract her from the task at hand, but she also has a voice inside of her that is a temptation, wafting her away from the true path. In Lily's case, the true path is to ascertain the truth about her mother. Lily wants so passionately to reveal the truth to August about who she is and why she has arrived, but something is increasing her resistance. August says, " 'You know, don't you, that the two of us need to have a good talk. And this time not about me. About you'" (Kidd 152).

"'I suppose,' I answered.

'What about right now?'

'Not right now'" (Kidd 152).

Although Lily wants August to know the truth, there is one little voice inside her head telling her that she cannot do that because she is not ready to comes to terms with reality quite yet.

After finally eliminating this distracting voice, Lily finds out who her mother was, why she knew August, and why she had left. "T.Ray had told me she came back for her things. But she'd come back for me, too. She'd wanted to bring me here, to Tiburon, to August's" (254). Lily achieves atonement with her mother here and forgives her when she realizes that her mother did love her after all. The same quote can be used to describe Lily's ultimate boon. Lily also realizes here that her mother did not leave her, but was actually planning to bring Lily into a new and better life with her. Lily had someone that truly loved her, and to her, that is all that she ever needed to know. Ever since the night that T. Ray told Lily that her mother never cared about her, Lily nearly went insane wondering if T. Ray was telling the truth. What if her mother never did love her? Knowing that somebody actually did provided her with the self-confidence necessary to maintain her journey.

The last section of Campbell's monomyth structure is the departure. Within this final chapter, Lily succeeds in her journey to find out information about her mother. The first part of the departure is the refusal of the return. T. Ray finds Lily at the Boatwrights, barges in on her blissful life, and insists that she come home with him. Lily's refusal of the return is when she rejects this unappealing offer. She tells him this firmly, yet he does not allow her to stay with August. In Campbell's "the rescue from without", August and the Daughters of Mary step in and allow Lily stand up to her father. August tells T .Ray that Lily is welcome to stay with her. Also, August and Rosaleen call and gather all the Daughters of Mary: "The front door opened, and Queenie, Violet, Lunelle, and Maybelee stumbled into the house, all wound up and looking like they had their clothes on backwards" (297). The Daughters knew Lily was in trouble and they had come to rescue her from T.Ray.

Lily finally crosses the return threshold when T.Ray allows her to stay with August. 'Good riddance' is all he says to her upon her final departure from his life. He does not give her a hug or show any sign of compassion when he gives his daughter over to a complete stranger. After crossing the return threshold, Lily becomes the master of two worlds when she conquers her unconscious and her persona. In terms of Jung, this is an enormous step for a person to jump. She becomes aware of herself and does not care about what others think of her. When Lily and her friend go to visit Zach at his school with all white people, they are made fun of for wanting to be with him. "We have reputations as 'nigger lovers,' which is how it is put to us, and when the ignoramuses ball up their notebook paper and throw it at Zach in the hallway...Becca and I are just as likely to get popped in the head as he is. Zach says we should walk on the other side of the hall from him. We say, 'Balled-up notebook paper- big deal'"(301). Not only does Lily not care about being called a "nigger lover," but also she is willing to take a hit or two for her friend. She has grown tremendously throughout the novel and has finally mastered her two worlds. At the end, Lily receives the freedom to live.

Lily begins the novel without any solid parental archetypes; however, throughout her journey she gains many maternal role models: "I go back to that one moment when I stood in the driveway with small rocks and clumps of dirt around my feet and looked back at the porch. And there they were. All these mothers. I have more mothers than any eight girls off the street. They are the moons shining over me" (302). Lily succeeds on her quest to find information about her mother, and she also succeeds in realizing much more. She gains a family that was definitely needed and wanted. She loves her new family with all her heart, and she knows they love her unconditionally.

Joseph Campbell's theory of the monomyth is evident throughout The Secret Life of Bees, and it demonstrates the depth of the hero's journey. It is apparent how Lily goes through each of the three phases and lucratively fulfills her main aspiration. The archetypes can also be seen in the progression of the story, and it can be said that Lily even realizes the Self during her journey. Sue Monk Kidd's novel is just one of the many works that can be understood within the monomyth because of its precise development and universal meaning.

Essay: The Role of Nature in The Secret Life of Bees

by Anonymous
March 15, 2008

In The Secret Life of Bees by Sue Monk Kidd, Lily feels lost without a mother to lead her step by step through life. However, with her escape to Tiburon, Lily finally finds support and consolation through new experiences and exposures. Specifically, Lily is able to discover an alternative mother figure: nature. Unlike her mother, nature is not a fleeting presence or a mere wisp of a memory. Lily finds inner peace and comfort in nature, since it is always present and constantly renewing itself, a trait that Lily never found in her mother.

Deborah is absent through most of Lily's life, a fleeting figure. Lily asks T-Ray about her mother and is disappointed: "I did manage to get a few scraps of information from him… my mother was buried in Virginia where her people came from. I got worked up at that, thinking I'd found a grandmother. No, he tells me, my mother was an only child whose mother died four years ago" (13). Lily's lack of a grandmother further emphasizes her mother's absence, since even the closest family connections to Deborah are nonexistent. Lily comments about missing her mother, "The oddest things caused me to miss her. Like training bras. Who was I going to ask about that?" (13). For a long time, Lily has not had a mother to physically attend to her needs and guide her through life. Even the small things, such as training bras, remind her everyday of her mother's absence. Lily is often confused and unsure about her mother, always reminded of her own ignorance: "I started thinking maybe I should find out what I could about my mother… But where to start? The night seemed like an ink blot I had to figure out. I sat there and studied the darkness, trying to see through it to some sliver of light" (101). Lily's thoughts about her mother are like muddled "ink blots"; she is often perturbed by how little she knows, and is constantly reminded of the times she never spent with her mother, never finding any leads to her mother's true self. From her days with T-Ray to her days in Tiburon, Lily is always aware of the briefness of Deborah's life.

Lily describes the nightmare about her mother as a cockroach as follows: "If I told you right now that I never wondered about that dream, never closed my eyes and pictured her with roach legs… with her worst nature, exposed, I would be… lying. A roach is a creature no one can love, but you cannot kill it. It will go on and on and on. Just try to get rid of it." (175) Since Lily has been separated from her mother for so long, she feels blind to her mother's true faults. Her doubts and questions "go on and on and on" and continue to bother her in the back of her mind. Deborah appears as a cockroach, with the identity of a stranger and an unfamiliar pest. Lily scrutinizes her mother's picture before her journey to Tiburon: "You could not believe the stories I saw in that picture… I laid the photograph beside my eighth-grade picture and examined every possible similarity" (13). Lily takes what little information she has about her mother and tries to extract any guesses or images about her mother's personality. She cannot grasp her mother's true personality, and therefore is always unsure and doubting. Lily's insecurities stem from the fact that she doesn't fully understand her mother, instead taking guesses and never standing on stable ground.

Conversely, nature is present throughout Lily's life as a continually replenished and renewed force, unlike Lily's mother. Lily describes the scene of the water fight, recalling: "Squirrels and Carolina wrens hopped as close as they dared and drank from the puddles and you could almost see the blades of brown grass lift themselves up and turn green" (168). In Tiburon, Lily begins to notice the cycle of rebirth in nature. Even in the scorching heat of the summer, the grass can grow again and renew itself with its limited resources. Lily notices that nature continues to live on in difficult circumstances. Lily also states, reflecting on May's death after Mary Day: "You could die in a river, but maybe you could get reborn in it, too, like the beehive tombs August had told me about" (229). Despite the recent death of May, Lily recognizes the river as an unbroken cycle of life rather than a destructive force. Nature is a consistent and constant force in Lily's life, continuing to thrive no matter the circumstances.

Meanwhile, Lily finds peace and comfort in the continuity of nature. Lily reflects on the river after May's death: "I wanted the river. Its wildness. I wanted to… suck river stones the way I'd done that night Rosaleen and I'd slept by the creek. Even May's death had not ruined the river for me. The river had done its best… to give May a peaceful ride out of this life" (229). Lily is comforted by the river during a time of grieving, knowing it will continue to flow as it always has. Lily depends on the river as a source of retreat and consolation, since it remains consistent despite the ravages of time. In another one of Lily's nightmares, she envisions nature falling apart: "In my dream…. I could see a huge, round moon in the sky… Next I heard a sound like ice breaking, and, looking up, saw the moon crack apart and start to fall. I had to run for my life. I woke with my chest hurting. I searched for the moon and found it in all in one piece, still spilling light over the creek" (54). Lily wakes up in a panic because nature, her consolation and comfort, disintegrates in her dream. She has long been dependent on nature, and when it disappears in a dream, Lily is fearful and insecure once again. Nature is a needed support system, a balm, a shield.

By the end of the book, nature becomes an unwavering and long-lasting mother figure for Lily, replacing Deborah. Gradually, Lily learns to find love, comfort and support in everyday events in her life, ranging from bee keeping to wading in a river. Consolation and emotional support come to her in other forms. In addition, nature teaches Lily to thrive and live on despite difficult circumstances, allowing her to accept the truth of her mother and create a unique identity for herself in the midst of racial prejudice.

Quiz 1

1. **In what year does the book begin?**
   A. 1972.
   B. 1964.
   C. 1968.
   D. 1946.

2. **What tragic event befell Lily at the young age of four?**
   A. She sufferred a knee injury.
   B. Her father died.
   C. Her mother died.
   D. She was abandoned.

3. **Where does the Owens family live?**
   A. Sylvan, South Carolina.
   B. McClellanville, South Carolina.
   C. Charlotte, North Carolina.
   D. Charleston, South Carolina.

4. **When was Rosaleen born?**
   A. 1909.
   B. 1919.
   C. 1964.
   D. She does not know for sure.

5. **Which teacher gave Lily the idea that she should aspire to do more than go to beauty school?**
   A. Mr. Posey.
   B. Mr. Gerald.
   C. Mr. Gaston.
   D. Mrs. Henry.

6. **Where was Rosaleen headed when she got into an altercation with the white men?**
   A. To get the medicine she needed.
   B. To buy groceries for the family.
   C. To register to vote.
   D. To go to community college.

7. **What did Lily want for her fourteenth birthday?**
    A. A new dog.
    B. A charm bracelet.
    C. A trip to Tiburon, South Carolina.
    D. Her mother's gloves.

8. **What is T. Ray's punishment for Lily?**
    A. Lashings.
    B. No dinner.
    C. Standing against a tree.
    D. Kneeling on grits.

9. **Where did Lily find her mother's belongings?**
    A. In the orchard.
    B. In the peach stand.
    C. In the attic.
    D. Under her bed.

10. **What did Lily do to pass time in the peach stand?**
    A. Listen to music.
    B. Read books.
    C. Write poems.
    D. Paint.

11. **Why did Rosaleen practice writing her name over and over in cursive?**
    A. She was entering school.
    B. She wanted to sign a letter.
    C. She was signing the deed to a house.
    D. It was a requirement to register to vote.

12. **What action landed Rosaleen in jail?**
    A. She yelled "fire" in a crowded theater.
    B. She assaulted a police officer.
    C. She poured spit from her snuff jug across white men's shoes.
    D. She kidnapped Lily.

13. **What was the nickname of the policeman who took Rosaleen and Lily to jail?**
    A. Sleeve.
    B. Shoe.
    C. Sock.
    D. Shirt.

14. **How did Lily sneak Rosaleen out of the hospital?**
    A. She called pretending to be a jailer's wife.
    B. She sprayed mace in the faces of the jailers.
    C. She pretended to be Rosaleen's daughter.
    D. She climbed out the window.

15. **Why did Lily want to go to Tiburon?**
    A. She found the name of the city engraved on the back of something that belonged to her mother.
    B. She studied Tiburon in school.
    C. Her mother was born in Tiburon.
    D. Her grandparents live in Tiburon.

16. **What was the method Lily used to look for a sign?**
    A. Take a walk and read the first word she sees.
    B. Look for symbols in her dreams.
    C. Close her eyes and listen to the first sound she hears.
    D. Take nine steps and look up.

17. **Where did Lily first find Black Madonna Honey?**
    A. The pink house.
    B. Frogmore Stew General Store and Restaurant.
    C. In the grocery store in Sylvan.
    D. In her attic.

18. **What did Lily steal for Rosaleen?**
    A. Red Rose snuff.
    B. Ointment for her head.
    C. Coca-Cola.
    D. A bra.

19. **What state is August Boatwright from?**
    A. Alabama.
    B. North Carolina.
    C. South Carolina.
    D. Virginia.

20. **How did August come to own the land where she keeps bees?**
    A. She grew up on the land.
    B. It was left to her by her grandfather.
    C. She and her sisters all pooled their money to buy the land.
    D. She bought it from a landowner in town.

21. **What was June's prior career?**
    A. She performed in an orchestra.
    B. She taught in an all-black high school.
    C. She sold peaches.
    D. She was a dentist.

22. **Which two of the Boatwright sisters were twins?**
    A. April and June.
    B. June and August.
    C. May and June.
    D. April and May.

23. **Why is June hesitant to accept Neil's marriage proposal?**
    A. Neil cheated on her with a woman from town.
    B. June's parents went through a bitter divorce.
    C. June did not believe in marriage.
    D. She was engaged before, and her fiance did not show up for the wedding.

24. **Who was not a member of the Daughters of Mary?**
    A. Cressie.
    B. Lunelle.
    C. Rose.
    D. Otis.

25. **According to the story of Our Lady of Chains, who found the statue?**
    A. A slave.
    B. A business man.
    C. A priest.
    D. A pregnant woman.

Quiz 1 Answer Key

1. **(B)** 1964.
2. **(C)** Her mother died.
3. **(A)** Sylvan, South Carolina.
4. **(D)** She does not know for sure.
5. **(D)** Mrs. Henry.
6. **(C)** To register to vote.
7. **(B)** A charm bracelet.
8. **(D)** Kneeling on grits.
9. **(C)** In the attic.
10. **(C)** Write poems.
11. **(D)** It was a requirement to register to vote.
12. **(C)** She poured spit from her snuff jug across white men's shoes.
13. **(B)** Shoe.
14. **(A)** She called pretending to be a jailer's wife.
15. **(A)** She found the name of the city engraved on the back of something that belonged to her mother.
16. **(D)** Take nine steps and look up.
17. **(B)** Frogmore Stew General Store and Restaurant.
18. **(A)** Red Rose snuff.
19. **(D)** Virginia.
20. **(B)** It was left to her by her grandfather.
21. **(B)** She taught in an all-black high school.
22. **(D)** April and May.
23. **(D)** She was engaged before, and her fiance did not show up for the wedding.
24. **(C)** Rose.
25. **(A)** A slave.

Quiz 2

1. **What stopped Lily the first time she attempted to touch the heart of Our Lady?**
   A. August pulled her hand away.
   B. A bee stung her.
   C. June stopped playing her cello.
   D. She tripped.

2. **Who was the first black male whom Lily found handsome?**
   A. She never found a black male to be handsome.
   B. Zachary Taylor.
   C. Otis Hill.
   D. Neil.

3. **Who is Willifred Merchant?**
   A. A dancer.
   B. A singer.
   C. A writer.
   D. A painter.

4. **What is the reason Rosaleen gives for moving into the pink house?**
   A. May gets scared at night by herself.
   B. Lily snores too loudly.
   C. Rosaleen is scared of bees.
   D. The cot in the honey house hurts Rosaleen's back.

5. **What does June throw at Neil's car when she gets mad at him?**
   A. Bananas.
   B. Tomatoes.
   C. Honey.
   D. Cheese.

6. **What did Zach give Lily as a gift?**
   A. A beeswax candle that he made.
   B. Flowers.
   C. A notebook.
   D. A ring.

7. **What happened during each of the Boatwrights' special months when they were children?**
    A. They didn't have to do chores.
    B. They got to eat their favorite foods.
    C. They got to stay up late.
    D. All of the above.

8. **What is a favorite dessert shared by August and Lily?**
    A. Chocolate cake.
    B. Peanuts in Coke.
    C. Honey cake.
    D. Ice cream sundaes.

9. **Why do women make the best beekeepers?**
    A. They can love creatures that sting.
    B. They are able to sing the bees to sleep.
    C. They smell sweet like flowers.
    D. They are able to care for many creatures at once.

10. **What did the Boatwright sisters' mother do professionally?**
    A. She worked in a hotel laundry.
    B. She taught high school.
    C. She was a dentist.
    D. She kept bees.

11. **What did the Boatright sisters' father do professionally?**
    A. He was a writer.
    B. He was a shoe salesman.
    C. He was a dentist.
    D. He was a beekeeper.

12. **Who decided to paint the Boatwright house bright pink?**
    A. August.
    B. Deborah.
    C. May.
    D. June.

13. **What celebrity was rumored to be coming to Tiburon?**
    A. Malcolm X.
    B. Jack Palance.
    C. Willifred Merchant.
    D. John F. Kennedy.

14. **Why did Lily want to go with Zach to visit the lawyer?**
    A. To ask the lawyer if he would represent her and Rosaleen.
    B. To spend time with Zach and to broaden her horizons.
    C. To ask the lawyer if he knew her mother.
    D. To try to get a job working for the lawyer.

15. **What was T. Ray's response when Lily called home?**
    A. Remorse.
    B. Happiness.
    C. Anger.
    D. Relief.

16. **What did Lily ask T. Ray when she spoke to him on the phone?**
    A. Do you know what my favorite color is?
    B. Why do you treat me the way you do?
    C. Do you love me?
    D. What really happened to my mother?

17. **What book did Attorney Clayton Forrest give to Zachary?**
    A. Basic Civil Rights Law.
    B. Black's Law Dictionary.
    C. South Carolina Legal Reports 1889.
    D. Constitutional Law.

18. **How did Lily dodge Forrest's questions about her past?**
    A. She pretended to faint.
    B. She said she had female problems.
    C. She vomited.
    D. She ran back into the truck.

19. **What was the basis of Lily's letter to T. Ray?**
    A. A father's day card she had given him.
    B. A song that June wrote.
    C. A poem she had read.
    D. The way the bees treat each other.

20. **What did Lily do with the letter she wrote to T. Ray?**
    A. She locked it in a drawer in the honey house.
    B. She mailed it.
    C. She buried it.
    D. She tore it up.

21. **What would Lily do after prayers when she forgot how to cross herself?**
    A. Put her hands in prayer positions.
    B. Fold her hands.
    C. Put her hands by her sides.
    D. Put her hand over her heart.

22. **Why did Lily and August have to water the bees?**
    A. They did not drape the hives.
    B. They forgot to feed the bees the day before.
    C. It was over 100 degrees outside.
    D. They forgot to put the hives in the shade.

23. **On what part of her body did Lily get stung?**
    A. Her face.
    B. Her ankle.
    C. Her wrist.
    D. Her stomach.

24. **What event allowed June and Lily to begin to become friends?**
    A. Zachary was put in jail.
    B. Mary's Days.
    C. May's death.
    D. A water fight.

25. **It is practically the law to do what when the temperature goes above 104 degrees?**
   A. Go to bed.
   B. Go inside.
   C. Have a water fight.
   D. Swim.

Quiz 2 Answer Key

1. **(C)** June stopped playing her cello.
2. **(B)** Zachary Taylor.
3. **(C)** A writer.
4. **(A)** May gets scared at night by herself.
5. **(B)** Tomatoes.
6. **(C)** A notebook.
7. **(D)** All of the above.
8. **(B)** Peanuts in Coke.
9. **(A)** They can love creatures that sting.
10. **(A)** She worked in a hotel laundry.
11. **(C)** He was a dentist.
12. **(C)** May.
13. **(B)** Jack Palance.
14. **(B)** To spend time with Zach and to broaden her horizons.
15. **(C)** Anger.
16. **(A)** Do you know what my favorite color is?
17. **(C)** South Carolina Legal Reports 1889.
18. **(B)** She said she had female problems.
19. **(A)** A father's day card she had given him.
20. **(D)** She tore it up.
21. **(D)** Put her hand over her heart.
22. **(C)** It was over 100 degrees outside.
23. **(C)** Her wrist.
24. **(D)** A water fight.
25. **(A)** Go to bed.

Quiz 3

1. **What memory did Lily have that connected her mother to the Boatwright house?**

   A. She recalled that T. Ray said that her mother loved honey.

   B. T. Ray said that Lily's mother would create paths for bugs using graham crackers and marshmallows.

   C. She remembered her mother humming a song that June played on her cello.

   D. She remembered T. Ray referring to Mary as "Our Lady of Chains."

2. **Who was the first person in Tiburon whom Lily asked about her mother?**

   A. August.

   B. May.

   C. Zach.

   D. June.

3. **Which boy threw his cola bottle, which landed all of the boys in jail?**

   A. Jackson.

   B. Zach.

   C. Neil.

   D. Lily.

4. **Why did it take so long to get Zach out of jail?**

   A. Judge Monroe was out of town.

   B. Clayton Forrest wouldn't help.

   C. It was peak honey season.

   D. The paperwork took too long to process.

5. **Lily referred to August as which part of Mary's body?**

   A. The fist.

   B. The eyes.

   C. The heart.

   D. The mouth.

6. **Lily referred to Rosaleen as which part of Mary's body?**

   A. The feet.

   B. The fist.

   C. The heart.

   D. The mouth.

7. **Which Boatwright sister was not told about Zach's arrest?**
  A. August.
  B. May.
  C. All of them.
  D. June.

8. **What question did Zach ask Lily when she went to visit him in jail?**
  A. Why didn't you help me?
  B. When will you come back?
  C. Have you been writing in your notebook?
  D. Do you love me?

9. **How did May find out about Zach's arrest?**
  A. Zach's mother called the Boatwright house.
  B. She read it in the paper.
  C. She saw it on the television news.
  D. She saw his face on a poster.

10. **When the Boatwright house went looking for May, what was the first clue that something was wrong?**
  A. The rocks from the wailing wall were all shattered.
  B. The bow from her hair was in a tree.
  C. Her flashlight was on the ground.
  D. Her shoes were found in the river.

11. **After May's death, what did Lily tell the police about her background?**
  A. She mixed up her lies and told a new fake story about her parents.
  B. She confessed the truth.
  C. She stuck with her made-up story about being an orphan.
  D. She said the Boatwrights had adopted her.

12. **How does Rosaleen tell the policeman that she and August are related?**
  A. August is Rosaleen's sister.
  B. August is Rosaleen's husband's first cousin.
  C. August is Rosaleen's step-sister.
  D. August is Rosaleen's third cousin.

13. **What is Zach's reaction to May's death?**
   A. He confesses his love for Lily.
   B. He spends all night at the wailing wall.
   C. He feels guilty that his being jailed caused her death.
   D. He falls into a deep depression and locks himself away.

14. **What is the second part of the beekeeping initiation?**
   A. Beekeeping without a helmet.
   B. Selling one jar of honey.
   C. Beekeeping blindfolded.
   D. Learning the story of Aristaeus.

15. **Where did August find May's suicide note?**
   A. In June's cello.
   B. In a bowl of bananas.
   C. In the wailing wall.
   D. Between the roots of a tree.

16. **How does August interpret May's suicide note?**
   A. She tells June to marry Neil.
   B. She adopts Lily.
   C. She tells Lily to go home.
   D. She decides to give up beekeeping.

17. **What does Mary Day celebrate?**
   A. Mary's marriage.
   B. The day when Mary rose to heaven.
   C. The day Mary realized she was pregnant.
   D. Mary's birth.

18. **Who named Mary Day?**
   A. August.
   B. May.
   C. June.
   D. April.

19. **What is Lily's reaction to Zach's kiss?**
    A. She pulls away.
    B. She tells on him to August.
    C. She loves it.
    D. She throws up.

20. **What is Zach's promise to Lily?**
    A. He will take her away from T. Ray.
    B. He will make something of himself, come back and be with her.
    C. He will never forget her.
    D. He will find out about her mother's past.

21. **What does Zach give Lily as a reminder of his promise?**
    A. A dog tag.
    B. A beeswax candle.
    C. A lock of his hair.
    D. A jar of honey.

22. **What does Lily notice is being handed to Mary by the angel Gabriel, in all of August's pictures?**
    A. A drop of honey.
    B. A beeswax candle.
    C. A bee.
    D. A lily.

23. **What is August's reaction to seeing Lily's photo of her mother?**
    A. She knows exactly who the woman is.
    B. She has no idea who is in the picture.
    C. She is extremely surprised.
    D. She has a faint memory of seeing the woman in the photo.

24. **How did August meet Deborah Fontanel Owens?**
    A. They did business together.
    B. August was Deborah's teacher.
    C. August was a housekeeper in Deborah's house.
    D. August picked up Deborah when Deborah was hitchhiking.

25. **Why did June resent Deborah Owens?**
    A. She couldn't get over August being a maid in her house.
    B. Deborah did not follow the customs of Our Lady.
    C. She squatted in the honey house for a long time.
    D. She did not understand why she left Lily.

Quiz 3 Answer Key

1. **(B)** T. Ray said that Lily's mother would create paths for bugs using graham crackers and marshmallows.
2. **(B)** May.
3. **(A)** Jackson.
4. **(A)** Judge Monroe was out of town.
5. **(C)** The heart.
6. **(B)** The fist.
7. **(B)** May.
8. **(C)** Have you been writing in your notebook?
9. **(A)** Zach's mother called the Boatwright house.
10. **(C)** Her flashlight was on the ground.
11. **(C)** She stuck with her made-up story about being an orphan.
12. **(B)** August is Rosaleen's husband's first cousin.
13. **(C)** He feels guilty that his being jailed caused her death.
14. **(D)** Learning the story of Aristaeus.
15. **(D)** Between the roots of a tree.
16. **(A)** She tells June to marry Neil.
17. **(B)** The day when Mary rose to heaven.
18. **(B)** May.
19. **(C)** She loves it.
20. **(B)** He will make something of himself, come back and be with her.
21. **(A)** A dog tag.
22. **(D)** A lily.
23. **(A)** She knows exactly who the woman is.
24. **(C)** August was a housekeeper in Deborah's house.
25. **(A)** She couldn't get over August being a maid in her house.

Quiz 4

1. **How old was Deborah when August met her?**
    A. Sixteen.
    B. Fourteen.
    C. Four.
    D. Three.

2. **What was the name of Deborah's imaginary friend?**
    A. Tica Tee.
    B. Melissa.
    C. Sweetie.
    D. Lily.

3. **What was Deborah's mother's name?**
    A. Mary.
    B. Lily.
    C. Sarah.
    D. Rachel.

4. **How long did August work for the Fontanel family?**
    A. One year.
    B. Nine years.
    C. Six months.
    D. Twenty years.

5. **What age was Deborah when August moved to South Carolina?**
    A. Thirty.
    B. Nineteen.
    C. Nine.
    D. Twenty-five.

6. **What happened to Deborah's father?**
    A. He had an affair with the maid before August.
    B. He died when Deborah was a baby.
    C. He left the family when Deborah was ten.
    D. He divorced Sarah before Deborah was born.

7. **Why did Deborah move to Sylvan?**
    A. She met T. Ray in college.
    B. She ended up there after hitchhiking.
    C. She found a job selling peaches.
    D. A friend from high school convinced her.

8. **Why did Deborah finally accept T. Ray's marriage proposal?**
    A. She had no money.
    B. She was pregnant.
    C. She took August's advice.
    D. She realized she truly loved T. Ray.

9. **Why didn't Deborah bring Lily to the Boatwrights?**
    A. Lily would be difficult in the honey house.
    B. She was depressed and falling apart.
    C. Lily couldn't stand the long busride.
    D. Deborah couldn't afford to bring Lily.

10. **Who told August that Deborah had died?**
    A. Rosaleen.
    B. The police.
    C. T. Ray.
    D. The Owens' neighbor.

11. **What important event was going on during the time of the novel?**
    A. The Fall of the Berlin Wall.
    B. The Disintegration of the Soviet Union.
    C. The Civil Rights Movement.
    D. The Civil War.

12. **How does Lily deal with her anger after learning about her mother from August?**
    A. She punches a pillow.
    B. She trashes the honey house.
    C. She calls T. Ray and yells.
    D. She runs away.

13. **How does Lily wake up following Mary Day?**
    A. Zach kisses her.
    B. She smells cakes.
    C. Rosaleen shakes her awake.
    D. August yells at her.

14. **Who helped look after Lily during the first few months after Deborah died?**
    A. August.
    B. Brother Gerald.
    C. Rosaleen.
    D. Mrs. Watson.

15. **Who cleans up the honey house?**
    A. August and June.
    B. Rosaleen and Lily.
    C. Zach and Lily.
    D. August and Rosaleen.

16. **What do the Daughters bathe in honey on Mary Day?**
    A. The statue of Our Lady.
    B. The pink house.
    C. The honey house.
    D. Lily.

17. **What is the symbolism of bathing something in honey?**
    A. Honey is sweet.
    B. Honey is made from bees.
    C. Honey is sticky.
    D. Honey is a preservative.

18. **What does Lily say would be the one Bible miracle she'd like to have happen to her?**
    A. To turn water into wine.
    B. Immaculate conception.
    C. To survive a great flood.
    D. To be raised from the dead.

19. **What does August bring with her when she visits Lily in the honey house?**
    A. A note from May.
    B. A small statue of Mary.
    C. A beeswax candle.
    D. Some of her mother's belongings.

20. **What is the piece of jewelry Lily receives that was her mother's?**
    A. A honeycomb necklace.
    B. A whale pin.
    C. A frog ring.
    D. A bee bracelet.

21. **Who does Lily think passed on the message to her mother that she needed a sign?**
    A. Rosaleen.
    B. May.
    C. T. Ray.
    D. Zach.

22. **What does Lily decide to carry around in her pocket every day?**
    A. May's note.
    B. Her mother's brush.
    C. A jar of honey.
    D. A pile of mouse bones.

23. **Where does Zach decide to go to high school in the fall?**
    A. South Carolina University.
    B. The black high school.
    C. The white high school.
    D. The local community college.

24. **When do bees loaf around?**
    A. When the moon is full.
    B. When their queen dies.
    C. When the temperature goes over 100.
    D. When it rains.

25. **What does T. Ray call Lily at the end of the novel?**
    A. Deborah.
    B. Daughter.
    C. Dear.
    D. Baby.

Quiz 4 Answer Key

1. **(C)** Four.
2. **(A)** Tica Tee.
3. **(C)** Sarah.
4. **(B)** Nine years.
5. **(B)** Nineteen.
6. **(B)** He died when Deborah was a baby.
7. **(D)** A friend from high school convinced her.
8. **(B)** She was pregnant.
9. **(B)** She was depressed and falling apart.
10. **(D)** The Owens' neighbor.
11. **(C)** The Civil Rights Movement.
12. **(B)** She trashes the honey house.
13. **(C)** Rosaleen shakes her awake.
14. **(D)** Mrs. Watson.
15. **(B)** Rosaleen and Lily.
16. **(A)** The statue of Our Lady.
17. **(D)** Honey is a preservative.
18. **(D)** To be raised from the dead.
19. **(D)** Some of her mother's belongings.
20. **(B)** A whale pin.
21. **(B)** May.
22. **(D)** A pile of mouse bones.
23. **(C)** The white high school.
24. **(B)** When their queen dies.
25. **(A)** Deborah.

ClassicNotes

GradeSaver™

Getting you the grade since 1999™

Other ClassicNotes from GradeSaver™

1984
Absalom, Absalom
Adam Bede
The Adventures of Augie
  March
The Adventures of
  Huckleberry Finn
The Adventures of Tom
  Sawyer
The Aeneid
Agamemnon
The Age of Innocence
The Alchemist (Coelho)
The Alchemist (Jonson)
Alice in Wonderland
All My Sons
All Quiet on the Western
  Front
All the King's Men
All the Pretty Horses
Allen Ginsberg's Poetry
The Ambassadors
American Beauty
And Then There Were
  None
Angela's Ashes
Animal Farm
Anna Karenina
Anthem
Antigone
Antony and Cleopatra
Aristotle's Ethics
Aristotle's Poetics
Aristotle's Politics
As I Lay Dying
As You Like It

Astrophil and Stella
Atlas Shrugged
Atonement
The Awakening
Babbitt
The Bacchae
Bartleby the Scrivener
The Bean Trees
The Bell Jar
Beloved
Benito Cereno
Beowulf
Bhagavad-Gita
Billy Budd
Black Boy
Bleak House
Bless Me, Ultima
Blindness
Blood Wedding
The Bloody Chamber
Bluest Eye
The Bonfire of the
  Vanities
The Book of the Duchess
  and Other Poems
The Book Thief
Brave New World
Breakfast at Tiffany's
Breakfast of Champions
The Brief Wondrous Life
  of Oscar Wao
The Brothers Karamazov
The Burning Plain and
  Other Stories
A Burnt-Out Case
By Night in Chile

Call of the Wild
Candide
The Canterbury Tales
Cat on a Hot Tin Roof
Cat's Cradle
Catch-22
The Catcher in the Rye
The Caucasian Chalk
  Circle
Charlotte Temple
Charlotte's Web
The Cherry Orchard
The Chocolate War
The Chosen
A Christmas Carol
Christopher Marlowe's
  Poems
Chronicle of a Death
  Foretold
Civil Disobedience
Civilization and Its
  Discontents
A Clockwork Orange
Coleridge's Poems
The Color of Water
The Color Purple
Comedy of Errors
Communist Manifesto
A Confederacy of
  Dunces
Confessions
Connecticut Yankee in
  King Arthur's Court
The Consolation of
  Philosophy
Coriolanus

For our full list of over 250 Study Guides, Quizzes,
Sample College Application Essays, Literature Essays and E-texts, visit:

www.gradesaver.com

ClassicNotes

GrⱯdeSaver™

Getting you the grade since 1999™

Other ClassicNotes from GradeSaver™

The Count of Monte
  Cristo
The Country Wife
Crime and Punishment
The Crucible
Cry, the Beloved
  Country
The Crying of Lot 49
The Curious Incident of
  the Dog in the
  Night-time
Cymbeline
Daisy Miller
David Copperfield
Death in Venice
Death of a Salesman
The Death of Ivan Ilych
Democracy in America
Devil in a Blue Dress
Dharma Bums
The Diary of a Young
  Girl by Anne Frank
Disgrace
Divine Comedy-I:
  Inferno
Do Androids Dream of
  Electric Sheep?
Doctor Faustus
  (Marlowe)
A Doll's House
Don Quixote Book I
Don Quixote Book II
Dora: An Analysis of a
  Case of Hysteria
Dr. Jekyll and Mr. Hyde
Dracula

Dubliners
East of Eden
Electra by Sophocles
The Electric Kool-Aid
  Acid Test
Emily Dickinson's
  Collected Poems
Emma
Ender's Game
Endgame
The English Patient
The Epic of Gilgamesh
Ethan Frome
The Eumenides
Everyman: Morality Play
Everything is Illuminated
The Faerie Queene
Fahrenheit 451
The Fall of the House of
  Usher
A Farewell to Arms
The Federalist Papers
Fences
Flags of Our Fathers
Flannery O'Connor's
  Stories
For Whom the Bell Tolls
The Fountainhead
Frankenstein
Franny and Zooey
The Giver
The Glass Castle
The Glass Menagerie
The God of Small Things
Goethe's Faust
The Good Earth

The Good Woman of
  Setzuan
The Grapes of Wrath
Great Expectations
The Great Gatsby
Grendel
The Guest
Gulliver's Travels
Hamlet
The Handmaid's Tale
Hard Times
Haroun and the Sea of
  Stories
Harry Potter and the
  Philosopher's Stone
Heart of Darkness
Hedda Gabler
Henry IV (Pirandello)
Henry IV Part 1
Henry IV Part 2
Henry V
Herzog
Hippolytus
The Hobbit
Homo Faber
House of Mirth
The House of the Seven
  Gables
The House of the Spirits
House on Mango Street
How the Garcia Girls
  Lost Their Accents
Howards End
A Hunger Artist
I Know Why the Caged
  Bird Sings

For our full list of over 250 Study Guides, Quizzes,
Sample College Application Essays, Literature Essays and E-texts, visit:

www.gradesaver.com

ClassicNotes

GradeSaver™

Getting you the grade since 1999™

Other ClassicNotes from GradeSaver™

I, Claudius
An Ideal Husband
Iliad
The Importance of Being
   Earnest
In Cold Blood
In Our Time
In the Time of the
   Butterflies
Inherit the Wind
An Inspector Calls
Into the Wild
Invisible Man
The Island of Dr. Moreau
Jane Eyre
Jazz
The Jew of Malta
Joseph Andrews
The Joy Luck Club
Julius Caesar
The Jungle
Jungle of Cities
Kama Sutra
Kate Chopin's Short
   Stories
Kidnapped
King Lear
King Solomon's Mines
The Kite Runner
Last of the Mohicans
Leaves of Grass
The Legend of Sleepy
   Hollow
A Lesson Before Dying
Leviathan
Libation Bearers

Life is Beautiful
Life of Pi
Light In August
Like Water for Chocolate
The Lion, the Witch and
   the Wardrobe
Little Women
Lolita
Long Day's Journey Into
   Night
Look Back in Anger
Lord Jim
Lord of the Flies
The Lord of the Rings:
   The Fellowship of the
   Ring
The Lord of the Rings:
   The Return of the
   King
The Lord of the Rings:
   The Two Towers
A Lost Lady
The Lottery and Other
   Stories
Love in the Time of
   Cholera
The Love Song of J.
   Alfred Prufrock
The Lovely Bones
Lucy
Macbeth
Madame Bovary
Maggie: A Girl of the
   Streets and Other
   Stories
Manhattan Transfer

Mankind: Medieval
   Morality Plays
Mansfield Park
The Marrow of Tradition
The Master and
   Margarita
MAUS
The Mayor of
   Casterbridge
Measure for Measure
Medea
Merchant of Venice
Metamorphoses
The Metamorphosis
Middlemarch
A Midsummer Night's
   Dream
Moby Dick
A Modest Proposal and
   Other Satires
Moll Flanders
Mother Courage and Her
   Children
Mrs. Dalloway
Much Ado About
   Nothing
My Antonia
Mythology
The Namesake
Native Son
Nickel and Dimed: On
   (Not) Getting By in
   America
Night
Nine Stories
No Exit

For our full list of over 250 Study Guides, Quizzes,
Sample College Application Essays, Literature Essays and E-texts, visit:

www.gradesaver.com

ClassicNotes

GradeSaver™

Getting you the grade since 1999™

Other ClassicNotes from GradeSaver™

Northanger Abbey
Notes from Underground
O Pioneers
The Odyssey
Oedipus Rex or Oedipus
  the King
Of Mice and Men
The Old Man and the Sea
Oliver Twist
On Liberty
On the Road
One Day in the Life of
  Ivan Denisovich
One Flew Over the
  Cuckoo's Nest
One Hundred Years of
  Solitude
Oroonoko
Oryx and Crake
Othello
Our Town
The Outsiders
Pale Fire
Pamela: Or Virtue
  Rewarded
Paradise Lost
A Passage to India
The Pearl
Percy Shelley: Poems
Perfume: The Story of a
  Murderer
Persepolis: The Story of
  a Childhood
Persuasion
Phaedra
Phaedrus

The Piano Lesson
The Picture of Dorian
  Gray
Poe's Poetry
Poe's Short Stories
Poems of W.B. Yeats:
  The Rose
Poems of W.B. Yeats:
  The Tower
The Poems of William
  Blake
The Poetry of Robert
  Frost
The Poisonwood Bible
Pope's Poems and Prose
Portrait of the Artist as a
  Young Man
Pride and Prejudice
The Prince
The Professor's House
Prometheus Bound
Pudd'nhead Wilson
Pygmalion
Rabbit, Run
A Raisin in the Sun
The Real Life of
  Sebastian Knight
Rebecca
The Red Badge of
  Courage
The Remains of the Day
The Republic
Rhinoceros
Richard II
Richard III

The Rime of the Ancient
  Mariner
Rip Van Winkle and
  Other Stories
The Road
Robinson Crusoe
Roll of Thunder, Hear
  My Cry
Romeo and Juliet
A Room of One's Own
A Room With a View
A Rose For Emily and
  Other Short Stories
Rosencrantz and
  Guildenstern Are
  Dead
Salome
The Scarlet Letter
The Scarlet Pimpernel
The Seagull
Season of Migration to
  the North
Second Treatise of
  Government
The Secret Life of Bees
The Secret River
Secret Sharer
Sense and Sensibility
A Separate Peace
Shakespeare's Sonnets
Shantaram
Short Stories of Ernest
  Hemingway
Short Stories of F. Scott
  Fitzgerald
Siddhartha

For our full list of over 250 Study Guides, Quizzes,
Sample College Application Essays, Literature Essays and E-texts, visit:

www.gradesaver.com

ClassicNotes

GradeSaver™

Getting you the grade since 1999™

Other ClassicNotes from GradeSaver™

Silas Marner
Sir Gawain and the
  Green Knight
Sister Carrie
Six Characters in Search
  of an Author
Slaughterhouse Five
Snow Falling on Cedars
The Social Contract
Something Wicked This
  Way Comes
Song of Roland
Song of Solomon
Songs of Innocence and
  of Experience
Sons and Lovers
The Sorrows of Young
  Werther
The Sound and the Fury
The Spanish Tragedy
Spenser's Amoretti and
  Epithalamion
Spring Awakening
The Stranger
A Streetcar Named
  Desire
Sula
The Sun Also Rises
Tale of Two Cities
The Taming of the Shrew
The Tempest
Tender is the Night
Tess of the D'Urbervilles
Their Eyes Were
  Watching God
Things Fall Apart

The Things They Carried
A Thousand Splendid
  Suns
The Threepenny Opera
Through the Looking
  Glass
Thus Spoke Zarathustra
The Time Machine
Titus Andronicus
To Build a Fire
To Kill a Mockingbird
To the Lighthouse
The Tortilla Curtain
Touching Spirit Bear
Treasure Island
Trifles
Troilus and Cressida
Tropic of Cancer
Tropic of Capricorn
Tuesdays With Morrie
The Turn of the Screw
Twelfth Night
Twilight
Ulysses
Uncle Tom's Cabin
Utopia
Vanity Fair
A Very Old Man With
  Enormous Wings
Villette
The Visit
Volpone
Waiting for Godot
Waiting for Lefty
Walden
Washington Square

The Waste Land
The Wealth of Nations
Where the Red Fern
  Grows
White Fang
A White Heron and
  Other Stories
White Noise
White Teeth
Who's Afraid of Virginia
  Woolf
Wide Sargasso Sea
Wieland
Winesburg, Ohio
The Winter's Tale
The Woman Warrior
Wordsworth's Poetical
  Works
Woyzeck
A Wrinkle in Time
Wuthering Heights
The Yellow Wallpaper
Yonnondio: From the
  Thirties
Zeitoun

For our full list of over 250 Study Guides, Quizzes,
Sample College Application Essays, Literature Essays and E-texts, visit:

www.gradesaver.com